Selections from

ROSSETTI & MORRIS

Selections from

ROSSETTI & MORRIS

EDITED

BY

H. M. BURTON, M.A.

CAMBRIDGE

AT THE UNIVERSITY PRESS

1939

CAMBRIDGE UNIVERSITY PRESS

Cambridge, New York, Melbourne, Madrid, Cape Town,
Singapore, São Paulo, Delhi, Tokyo, Mexico City

Cambridge University Press
The Edinburgh Building, Cambridge CB2 8RU, UK

Published in the United States of America by Cambridge University Press, New York

www.cambridge.org
Information on this title: www.cambridge.org/9781107692237

First published 1929
Reprinted 1939
First paperback edition 2011

A catalogue record for this publication is available from the British Library

ISBN 978-1-107-69223-7 Paperback

PREFACE

The arrangement of this Selection may need a word of explanation. Rossetti wrote little prose, and that little, although distinguished, is by general consent not deeply important. The one extract, therefore, from *Hand and Soul*, seemed to fall naturally at the end of the Selections from Rossetti, although published actually before most of the poems. With Morris, however, prose and verse marched side by side, particularly after about 1870, each equally important and typical of the author; a stricter chronological arrangement has therefore been observed in the Selections from Morris.

For permission to reproduce such poems by Rossetti as are still in copyright acknowledgement is due to Messrs Ellis, 29 New Bond Street; for similar permission in respect of copyright works by Morris I am indebted to the Trustees of William Morris's Estate and Messrs Longmans, Green and Co.

H. M. B.

June, 1929

CONTENTS

* Poems or passages marked with an asterisk are not printed complete.

WILLIAM MORRIS

    * Poems or passages marked with an asterisk are not printed complete.

INTRODUCTION

Dante Gabriel Rossetti (christened Gabriel Charles Dante) was born in London in 1828, the son of an exiled Italian patriot. After a period at King's College School he went, in 1846, to the 'antique' school at the Royal Academy, in pursuit of an early ambition (more substantially founded than most childish ambitions) to become an artist. The principles and practices of the Academy at that time represented everything against which he was shortly to rebel so actively, and it is not surprising that the chief things he acquired there were a reputation for waywardness and eccentricity, a mild contempt for his masters, and a few valuable friendships—notably those of Holman Hunt and Millais. It is certain that he never learnt to draw very well.

From this youthful friendship there grew, under the leadership, probably, of Holman Hunt, and by a process that is to this day vague and disputed, the so-called Pre-Raphaelite Brotherhood; but a full year before its official inception both Hunt and Rossetti had been working and studying along the lines that the Brotherhood's doctrines afterwards prescribed.

It is necessary here merely to mention this movement, since its aims applied to pictorial art rather than to literature. Art, since the beginning of the nineteenth century, had fallen upon evil days, days of imitation and emptiness, and, said the Brotherhood, it could only be rescued by the determination of artists to ignore the precepts of their masters and paint only what they saw, as they saw it. The small band (originally Hunt, Millais and Rossetti—although here again there is much dispute) decided that it was in Italian art of the fourteenth and fifteenth centuries that this faithfulness could be seen at its best, and that Raphael was the last of the school of original mediaeval painters. The name Pre-Raphaelite was adopted, therefore, as meaning 'before the imitators of Raphael,' but not before Raphael himself.

The members at first painted mediaeval subjects with a strict attention to detail and to colour. They increased their membership to seven, they signed their pictures with the letters P.R.B., they held monthly meetings and published a magazine (unhappily named *The Germ*) which duly failed. For a time their work was received with some respect by the critics; but in 1850 the meaning of the mystic letters leaked out, and, for reasons which only an intimate knowledge of the social and artistic history of the period can explain, the Brotherhood was attacked mercilessly and scandalously in all the journals, by all the writers. Just as, later on, Rossetti and Swinburne were to be lashed by Buchanan for their poetry, so Hunt, Millais and Rossetti were lashed by *The Times*, by Dickens in *Household Words*, by Macaulay, and by many others less important.

The effect on the Brotherhood was immediate and fatal. Millais subdued the fiercer originalities in his style and was able to discover a parallel line of development which was to prove more popular; Hunt adhered nobly to his principles and triumphed in the end over reaction; Rossetti withdrew almost completely from public exhibition. Two letters to *The Times* by Ruskin rebuked the critics and encouraged the artists. But Hunt went off to the Holy Land to paint Biblical pictures from the life, another member went to the goldfields, a third became a Roman Catholic and gave up painting, and so, as Rossetti remarked, when they saw Hunt off from the station, "the whole Round Table was dissolved."

2

However far the P.R.B. fell short of their aims and ideals they had done useful work for English art; for Rossetti, however, the movement in the end meant little. His painting (except for a very few pictures) grew less and less 'mediaeval' and more and more 'Rossetti'; his poetry had been 'mediaeval' from the start.

It has been said that a sort of pageant of the Middle Ages passed through the world of Victorian Literature; Tennyson watched it from his windows and described what he saw; Browning put on fancy dress and joined it; but Rossetti was already of it. Although he could be perfectly at home with English manners and customs when he wished, Rossetti was essentially a foreigner. His earliest recollections must have been of Italians in his father's house in London, plotting rebellion, and quarrelling over their plots. His father himself, dressed as an English sailor and marching in a squad, had been smuggled from Italy in time of rebellion by a friendly English Admiral. The old patriot, moreover, had been a voluminous writer and talker about Dante, whose works the children had known—but scarcely assimilated—from babyhood. It is not surprising, therefore, that when the brightest of them came to write and to paint his imagination turned to the Middle Ages, not with the loving care of the scholar or the pedant, but with the warmth, the sympathy, the *rightness* of one whose mind was already, in many respects, almost mediaeval. It is here, and here only, that the literary and artistic sides of Pre-Raphaelitism coincide; in both there are the interest in mediaeval themes and legends, the bright ingenuous colours of an age that had but newly discovered colour, the stark realities of an age that had not yet forgotten primitive cruelty. To speak strictly, there is no such thing as Pre-Raphaelite Literature, there are only literary Pre-Raphaelites; but if there could be a Pre-Raphaelite

3

Literature, these three—mediaevalism, colour and directness—would be its chief characteristics. These three, also, together with a careful love of detail which is also mediaeval, are the qualities which we shall find most insistent in the poetry of Rossetti.

Often in doubt as to which of the arts he would finally pursue, Rossetti turned for a while, after the disaster of the P.R.B., to poetry. He had already written *The Blessed Damozel*, *The Portrait* and other poems; some of his work had appeared in *The Germ*, and there were in manuscript a large number of translations from Dante. The attack on his paintings brought out his indolence, and he would lie on his back for hours composing verses. His father rallied him, and he took up his brushes once more; but meanwhile two important things were happening—his love for Elizabeth Siddal, and his friendship with Ruskin.

Miss Siddal, discovered in a milliner's shop by one of Rossetti's friends, became, by reason of her undisputed beauty, first his model, then his pupil, and finally, after ten years, his wife. The engagement was protracted by her ill-health and his inability to save money. Her beauty was of the type that Rossetti has made familiar—bright, copper-coloured hair, long, stately neck, languid eyes, full lips. She had undeniable gifts, combined with wretched health and little education, and it would seem that in view of Gabriel's careless habits, his impatience, and his superior mental and social training, the marriage must have been foredoomed. For nearly two years, however, they lived together on reasonably happy terms. Then she died from an overdose of laudanum, and Rossetti in his grief buried the manuscript of his poems with her.

The connection with Ruskin was never properly a friendship at all. The whole cast of mind and habit of life of the two were so different as to render a friendship between them impossible. Ruskin admired the other's work, although he criticised it freely, and—more important for the artist—he bought it. Also he was the soul of kindness to Miss Siddal, offering to pay her £150 a year for her drawings, whether she finished any or not. It is probable that at some time he was genuinely fond of Rossetti, but the latter's point of view seems most eloquently summed up in his expression of joy after Ruskin's first visit: "He seems in a mood to make my fortune!"

To oblige Ruskin, Rossetti conducted art-classes at the Working Men's College, and there he came into contact with Morris and Burne-Jones. They immediately fell under his sway, as people did all through his life. "I want to imitate Gabriel as much as I can," wrote Morris, one of the most strong-minded and self-opinionated of men; and Burne-Jones was even more humble. In 1857 they were all engaged in painting frescoes, for love, on the walls of the Union Society's Debating Hall at Oxford. Their knowledge of mural painting was inadequate, and their work did not last; but it was finely conceived and (Rossetti's share at least) finely executed, and it brought Rossetti into touch with an admiring circle of friends and critics at Oxford—among them Swinburne.

All the while the poet was steadily writing. He contributed to *The Oxford and Cambridge Magazine* (conducted by Morris and his friends) and by 1862 had collected enough verse for a volume. It was written in a neat little book given to him for the purpose by his wife—a trifling circumstance that may have helped the impulse to bury the book with her. In burying it, also, he was not untouched by remorse; the poems, he said, represented hours of enjoyment and of work that he might well have devoted to her in her suffering, and it was fitting that they should go with her. The noble action had a less noble sequel.

5

From 1862 to 1867 have been called his 'good years.' He painted some of his loveliest pictures—notably *Beata Beatrix* and *The Beloved*—and became famous and wealthy, living in a large house in Cheyne Walk, Chelsea, together with (at various times) Swinburne, George Meredith and his brother William—one of the fairest and most conscientious of biographers. There was a large garden where he kept queer animals as pets—a kangaroo, a deer, a racoon, a wombat (which once ate some valuable cigars), a bull, an armadillo and others, not all at the same time, of course. He collected bric-a-brac and blue china, he entertained his few friends lavishly, and on the whole, after his grief had softened, spent some of the happiest years of his life. But about 1867 he began to suffer from insomnia and to have fears for his sight. In 1868 he went to Scotland, where he recovered sufficiently to return to poetry, and where some of his finest poems were written in a cave by the side of a stream—the scene of *The Stream's Secret*. At the same time he was trying painfully to remember the poems lying in his wife's coffin. On his return to London he was persuaded to consent to their recovery. Permission was obtained from the Home Secretary, a fire was kindled by the graveside, and while Rossetti sat in anguish in a friend's house, the volume was recovered, soiled but not illegible.

By 1870 the poems were published. (The Translations from the Italian had appeared in 1862.) There was a chorus of praise from all sides; but then, as now, it was possible, if you were sufficiently influential, to arrange for your books to be reviewed by your friends, and the glowing tributes came from the pens of William Rossetti, Swinburne and Morris. They were none the less sincere and capable for that. A year later Robert Buchanan published, under the pseudonym Thomas Maitland, an article in the *Contemporary Review* called *The Fleshly School of Poetry*.

Rossetti, and to some extent Swinburne and Morris, were accused of coarseness and immorality, of considering the body as more important than the soul, and, most absurd of all, of being inartistic and second-rate poets. Actually, Rossetti's errors, like Swinburne's, had been of taste rather than of feeling. He had very little 'English reserve' in love matters (at least when it came to writing about them), and, as he himself pleaded, it was in emphasising the subservience of the corporal to the spiritual that he had written so frankly in certain sonnets. Nothing daunted, Buchanan reprinted the article in pamphlet form under his own name a year later. He was well known and popular, and his attack had supporters. Rossetti the sensitive, who had staked his reputation and his vanity on the volume, was wounded, and with the same instability that he had shown in 1850, he gave way before the onslaught.

Briefly, he collapsed. His insomnia grew worse, and drove him to chloral, a drug then believed to be harmless. From small doses he passed to incredibly large ones, and he very soon became completely dependent upon it. Here again it is necessary to be cautious in judging him. The drug almost certainly saved his reason in the first place; later it secured him just enough sleep by night to enable him to work by day. It is necessary to read an account of his life between 1867 and 1870 to realise what insomnia was doing for him. Chloral may have made his last years a tragedy; but it enabled him to give to the world paintings and poems as important as *Proserpine*, and *The King's Tragedy*.

But for a time there was no question of work. His brother, calling on him at Chelsea, found him, to his distress and amazement, 'past question not entirely sane.' He attempted suicide, he imagined the world against him in an organised conspiracy, he fancied he detected insults

7

from the best of his friends. Eventually he was got to Scotland where, under careful guidance, he gradually recovered and began spasmodically to work again.

But the end was not far. For two years he lived with the Morrises at Kelmscott, a home of peace and culture among beautiful scenery which he scarcely ever noticed. There he painted *Dante's Dream*, one of his most popular pictures, and wrote some fine sonnets. He left Kelmscott, characteristically because he thought some anglers had intentionally insulted him, and returned to Chelsea. The whole spirit of the house was changed; there were no more parties, most of his friends having been alienated by his suspicions and accusations; the famous blue china was sold; there were no more animals. For two years he lived in comparative seclusion, attended devotedly by Watts-Dunton, visited regularly by his brother, painting occasional replicas of his most famous pictures for immediate sale. Another breakdown was followed by a new spasm of work, and about 1879 he made the acquaintance of Mr (later Sir) Hall Caine. In 1881 the latter came to live in his house and tended him to the end with great patience and kindness. The same year a new volume of poems was published and favourably received. But Rossetti was too far gone in his depression and melancholia to care for appreciation. He was seized with a fit while staying at Birchington-on-Sea, and died there on Easter Day, 1882.

His character represents a confusing array of contradictions. Benson (*Rossetti: English Men of Letters* Series) summed it up thus: "Such then was Rossetti: mystical, full of passion, haunted by the sense of beauty, with an intense need of loving and being loved; dominant, fiery, genial, robust; with a narrow outlook, and yet with a keen intellectual power; capable, generous, lavish, humorous; a natural leader of men, self-centred, unbalanced; with

8

no touch of tranquillity about him, but eager, ardent, impatient." This would seem to say everything, and yet there are a few aspects that are somehow excluded.

He stays with a friend of W. B. Scott's, a kind old lady, not wealthy, in Scotland; she offers to lend him money, but he refuses, and tells Scott that he has refused; and yet at her death it is found that he has received at least £100 from her. Again, when the Morris decorating firm is being re-organised, and the original share-holders are being asked to renounce their interests, Rossetti affects complete indifference to his share of the capital; but he accepts it, to put it away for the ultimate benefit of one of the Morris family—and after his death it is discovered that he had made considerable inroads upon it! Or again, he is painting a calf at Finchley and cannot, or will not, afford the daily 'bus-fare; so he billets himself upon Madox Brown, who is poor, sleeps in the parlour until noon every day, wears Brown's great-coat incessantly whether Brown wants it or not, and, when delicately asked to go because Mrs Brown is ill, flatly refuses. He engages an assistant, Treffry Dunn, to mix his colours and prepare his canvases, and to this day it is not certain how much of the 'replica work' attributed to him is by the master, and how much by the servant. He is, at the best, inconsiderate to his wife who, feeble already, is (even Benson admits) wounded by his unfeeling conduct. In a tea-shop he loosens the hair of a country-girl, a stranger, because he wants to see what it looks like hanging down....

And yet he was loved, as well as admired, by everyone who knew him. Madox Brown wrote, when Rossetti had been trying to sell a picture for him, "never did fellow, I think, so bestir himself for a rival before; it is very good and very great to act so." Later in life, when Rossetti was in frequent ill-health, his friends' devotion was amazing.

9

They would meet and make plans for him, dividing the days and nights into periods for watching by him, giving up time and money and work to nurse him or to conduct him down to the country, knowing all the while that their reward would be groans and suspicions. No man inspires such devotion who has not more in him of good than of evil. In his youth he had possessed a large wholesome sense of fun, and even in his darker days it sometimes shone through. His talk was pointed and terse, seldom malicious. Always he was thoughtful and sympathetic for his friends, almost at the same time as he was imposing on them—just as he would borrow from one to lend to another, or draw upon a fund set aside for jewellery for his wife in order to help a widow and her children. It is easy, but unjust, to say briefly a "cad." Perhaps the best decision that can be based on the accounts of him which we possess is that he was morally unstable, full of good impulses that soon wore themselves out, easily discouraged, seeking too often the line of least resistance.

We shall look in vain among his works for 'nature' poems on the Wordsworth or Tennyson model, for classical excursions like Swinburne's *Atalanta*, for spontaneous personal lyrics like Shelley's. We shall find everywhere a keen sense of detail—not apparently relevant, and yet helping to build up an impression, just as little pieces of bric-a-brac appear time and again in his paintings. We shall find, too, a love of colour, of bright words and luminous pictures; a sense, also, of futility, of waste and despondency in all things, beauty squandered. Occasionally we shall meet that sudden enlightening phrase, or line, or inspiration that catches us up and brings us to a standstill before the thought, 'this is genius!' There is one such in *Jenny*:

> You know not what a book you seem,
> Half-read by lightning in a dream;

another in a sonnet (*A Superscription*):

> Sleepless with cold commemorative eyes;

and again in another sonnet the phrase "the devious coverts of dismay." But each must discover his jewels for himself.

Benson quotes the last two lines of *Love-lily* for the summary of Rossetti's philosophy of Love:

> Whose speech Truth knows not from her thought,
> Nor Love her body from her soul,

but Swinburne has a couplet in *Prelude* which is an apter summary of the whole range of Rossetti's verse:

> Delight whose germ grew never grain,
> And passion dyed in its own pain.

Of the faithful and graphic attention to detail we shall find ample evidence in the ballads. Perhaps the best example is in *The Bride's Prelude*. The atmosphere is hot and windless, so still that the girl

> Heard far beneath the plunge and float
> Of a hound swimming in the moat;

while earlier in the same poem is a stanza that suggests a mediaeval illuminated manuscript:

> Against the haloed lattice-panes
> The bridesmaid sunned her breast;
> Then to the glass turned tall and free,
> And braced and shifted daintily
> Her loin-belt through her cote-hardie.

The haze of sunlight about the lattice like a halo, the 'bracing' and 'shifting' of the girl's clothes, the exactness of their names—these are authentic details by a man accustomed to studying a model as he painted. Perhaps one of the finest examples of all occurs in *A Last Confession*; the girl has been stabbed and falls, and

> her stiff bodice scooped the sand
> Into her bosom.

We shall observe this insistence on dramatic detail again in considering *Woodspurge*.

A notable feature of the ballads is the suddenness with which we plunge into them:

> "Why did you melt your waxen man,
>> Sister Helen?"

and again:

> "Who rules these lands?" the Pilgrim said;
>> (*The Staff and Scrip*)

and

> "By none but me can the tale be told."
>> (*The White Ship*)

They are all long—many times as long as their mediaeval models—and nearly all have a touch of horror. They should, moreover, be read aloud; the refrain in *Sister Helen*, for example, when read silently, becomes a tiresome distraction; heard, it is an urgent and eloquent chorus, part of the story and at the same time a commentary.

Most of the sonnets belong to a sequence called *The House of Life*. They extol the darker and negative virtues—Youth, Hope, Patience in despair, and finally Hope again—and they insist (a little too emphatically for some tastes) on the essential sympathy between body and soul in love. The meaning is never very obscure, the philosophy seldom profound, but occasionally the poetry soars, as in *The Hill Summit*:

> This feast-day of the sun, his altar there
>> In the broad west has blazed for vesper-song;
>> And I have loitered in the vale too long
>> And gaze now a belated worshipper...

The general opinion is, however, that his finest complete poems are his earliest (apart from the *Juvenilia*, of course), *The Blessed Damozel* and *The Portrait*.

He owes little to any predecessor. There was a time when he, and all the Pre-Raphaelites, were held by Browning, and *A Last Confession* is in the manner of Browning's dramatic monologues; Tennyson's influence has also been observed in *The Portrait*; but the only obvious model is Keats. It is impossible to read *The Eve of St Agnes* or *The Eve of St Mark* without wondering whether Keats merely anticipated the Pre-Raphaelite cult of the mediaeval, or whether the later poets deliberately and devotionally (for they loved Keats) copied the

> Lucent syrops, tinct with cinnamon,

or the

> warm angled winter-screen,
> On which were many monsters seen,
> Called doves of Siam, Lima mice,
> And legless birds of Paradise,
> Macaw, and tender Avadavat,
> And silken-furred Angora cat.

From Keats, too, probably came the trick of coupling words (often uncomfortable yoke-fellows)—a trick of Swinburne's and of Morris's also—like 'wind-warm,' 'winter-bitten, angel-greeted door,' 'autumn-fall,' 'sphinx-faced.' It was a trick which grew on him with the years, and lost its force through its frequency; another trick was objectionable from the first—his atrocious rhymes. Many of them were poor ('free-will' and 'Evil' is surely the worst), but the weak feminine rhyme is the most annoying; again, it is a Pre-Raphaelite characteristic. 'Bare' and 'spring-water,' 'where' and 'quagwater,' 'of,' 'Love,' and 'enough,' 'breeze' and 'rushes' are all frequent or typical.

But if Swinburne and Morris and a few others share these weaknesses, in most respects Rossetti stands alone, and for

13

a very good reason. There is no poet in English Literature, on so important a level, who was also a great painter; there are probably few who were so insensitive to outside influences, either of education or of environment; and there is certainly no other who was, by birth, three parts Italian.

With WILLIAM MORRIS (1834–96) we pass to a very different problem. Where Rossetti attempted two arts and occasionally excelled in each, Morris's work embraced far more and always with success; where Rossetti was unstable as water, Morris was purposeful and firm as rock; where Rossetti was almost mediaeval in his thought and outlook, Morris was a keen and successful business-man of the nineteenth century, active in economic and social movements, and yet able to spirit himself and his reader back, as completely and unreservedly, to the Middle Ages. Yet there is enough in common between these two, even where they differed, to justify their inclusion in the same study. Morris may have called himself

Dreamer of dreams, born out of my due time,

(though the first half of the quotation is truer than the second), but the same may as truthfully have been said of Rossetti. Rossetti's thoughts may have been constantly in Italy of the fifteenth century; Morris's were as constantly in Northern Europe of an earlier age, or in ancient Greece; and yet both found time for contemporary interests— Rossetti's personal or artistic, Morris's economic or social. For two years, moreover, they were bound by an affectionate tie as master and pupil.

Morris was born of well-to-do parents at Walthamstow, near London. His boyhood was spent in Epping Forest, and there is an illuminating legend of his having possessed a toy suit of armour and gone riding about as a knight among the Essex hornbeams. At school at Marlborough he learnt little save details of nature and of archaeology from his long walks in the neighbourhood and his long browsings in the library. In 1853, being intended for the Church, he went to Exeter College, Oxford. At the same time, and the same college, entered Edward Burne-Jones, destined to be his closest friend through life.

To one whose interests lay in art and archaeology rather than in classical or mathematical scholarship the University had little to offer in those days. These two soon found themselves standing almost alone. They dreamed of a reformation in art, they tramped the Oxford lanes talking of the Middle Ages or sat late into the night reading Tennyson and Shakespeare. By degrees, with that mysterious impetus which we saw working among the Pre-Raphaelites, they gathered around them a small body of kindred spirits. They gave themselves a title—The Brotherhood—and eventually published a magazine—*The Oxford and Cambridge Magazine*.

At the age of twenty-one Morris inherited £900 a year, and it is eloquent of his seriousness that of all his plans for spending it none was for any selfish aim and all were for some ideal. Meanwhile both Morris and Burne-Jones had decided, walking on the sands at Dieppe one moonlit night, that the Church was not their vocation and that they would devote their lives to art. Morris became a pupil of Street, then an Oxford architect, in 1856, and continued to live in Oxford after taking his degree.

But he soon left Street's office in order to devote his time to the less exact arts. He had discovered, for example, that he could write verse, and it was not long after this discovery that *The Oxford and Cambridge Magazine* was founded. To this he contributed most of the funds and a good deal of the 'copy.' Poems, a few prose romances, and even a critical review appeared during the brief year of the magazine's existence, but already, before the year was over, his impetuous spirit had found other activities. His meeting with Rossetti has already been chronicled, and under the sway of Gabriel's personality, and of his dictum that 'everybody should paint,' he had even begun on a large picture of a subject from Malory. The painting of the Union frescoes took place in 1857, but already it was becoming evident that Morris's gifts lay in design and decoration rather than in 'easel-painting.' Even for the frescoes his inventiveness and his wide knowledge were more useful than his talent, for it was Morris (who never seemed to require to learn anything, but knew all that was necessary instinctively, as it were) who was able to decide what armour was relevant to the fresco and then to supervise its making.

During this year, also, the longer poems of *The Defence of Guenevere* were written, and the book appeared in 1858. It passed almost unnoticed in an age when Tennyson still ruled. Morris lingered in Oxford, nobly continuing with his painting, staying, moreover, to woo and to win Jane Burden, who became the faithful and affectionate 'Janey' Morris, whom Rossetti so frequently painted, and who remained the intimate friend of all the Pre-Raphaelite circle.

Apart from its intrinsic interest the marriage had amazing and reverberating results on the development not only of Morris himself but of all English domestic art and architecture. The day of the Adam brothers and of Hepplewhite was not only over, it was long forgotten; and the flatness and poverty that Rossetti had found in the Academy of 1846 Morris found in the domestic arts of 1857. It was one thing to marry a wife; a more difficult problem was to find a house in which a sensitive artist could live happily. When that search had failed, and a house had

16

been designed and built—in an orchard at Upton in Kent—the next difficulty was to furnish it. Morris soon found that English merchants had very little to offer him that he could tolerate, and with characteristic courage he set about making everything anew. Wall-paper was sketched, tiles painted, tables, chairs, pottery, glass, all were planned on lines of the simplest strength and beauty. Morris would draw up the designs, take them to the manufacturers, break down all opposition, and even supervise the actual work. The 'Red House' at Upton, "where ripe apples fell into the open windows on hot nights," became, after a few years, a home of beauty and of happiness. His two daughters were born there, and there, too, came all his friends, to play bowls on the lawn in the cool summer evenings and to fill the house to overflowing, so that even Swinburne would have to sleep on the floor. It was a very bitter blow when, in 1865, illness and financial stringency forced him to leave Upton and to return to London.

A third reason for living in London lay in the activities of a new firm, Morris, Marshall, Faulkner and Co., which had been founded a few years earlier. It had grown directly out of Morris's difficulties in finding furniture and hangings to please his tastes. Although there were several share-holders (including Rossetti, Madox Brown and Burne-Jones) there was little capital, and the work was carried out in small premises in London. At first the firm undertook little but church work, principally stained-glass windows, but its scope was soon widened and among the earliest productions were wall-papers and hangings designed by Morris. His share in the work, indeed, was always the largest and it was inevitable that the firm should eventually become Morris and Co., although this did not actually happen until 1875, and even then not without friction. The removal to London in 1865 freed him from the long and frequent journeys to town, and in the new-found leisure his thoughts returned to poetry. *The Life and Death of Jason*, published in 1867, was the result, and it immediately captured the public. This was encouraging after the failure of his first book, and Morris never again laid down his pen for so long a period. *The Earthly Paradise*, in three volumes, appeared between 1868 and 1870, and was just as popular. It is constructed on the scheme of the *Canterbury Tales* and the *Decameron* with two stories—one from the Classics and one from the non-classical mythology—for every month. Our present generation has never learnt the art of reading long poems, and it is a little difficult to re-create the enthusiasm that Morris aroused in the 'seventies. Yet all these stories are told with success. They may not constitute the finest narrative poetry in the language, but they come very near it; and once the original disinclination to settle down to poems of some thousands of lines has been overcome, there is no thought of laying them aside unfinished. The story is carried along almost without pause; even the uneventful passages that must occur in the daily life of the most heroic character are made attractive and stirring by sheer craftsmanship—for it was in craftsmanship, as we shall see, that Morris excelled.

Before *The Earthly Paradise* had been finished, his thoughts had turned to the Icelandic legends. The Sagas, the Epics of Northern Europe, comparable with the great Greek and Roman Epics, attracted Morris by their great and savage simplicity. He learnt Icelandic and translated some of the stories into prose, while another, *The Lovers of Gudrun*, appeared in *The Earthly Paradise*. His life at this period was as crowded as a man's life could be. To begin with, there was the firm, for which (apart from the

18

routine business of management, which would have been in itself a 'full-time job' for most men) he was constantly engaged in weaving, designing and drawing. At this time, too, he began to study the intricacies of the art (or science) of dyeing, and, in his spare time, took up the illumination of manuscripts. In 1871 he rented and furnished a new house at Kelmscott on the upper Thames, and in the same year embarked on a tour of several weeks in Iceland. On his return he published *Love is Enough*—a mystical sort of 'morality'—followed in a few years by *Three Northern Love-Stories* in prose and a verse translation of *The Aeneid*.

It is, of course, impossible not to be amazed at the enormous energy that made all these undertakings not only possible, but successful. Yet the seeming miracle is made a little more credible when we remember two or three things. In the first place, all these branches of art were, to Morris, but one art. To him a painted tile, a design for a chintz or a settle, a stained-glass window, a piece of dyed cloth, an illuminated capital in a book, a story, a poem—all were expressions of one and the same impulse. Secondly, the artist was Morris—a statement which explains itself just as does the physician's diagnosis at the time of his death: "his complaint was just that he was William Morris." To him the job in hand was more than his work, it was his recreation, and the soundest plank in his platform when later he entered politics as a Socialist was that there must always be enjoyment and pleasure in a man's daily work. Thirdly, this amazing man must always be occupied, and could usually do more than one thing at a time. At school he had spent his leisure hours weaving string patterns; later he complained that "if a chap can't compose an epic while he's weaving tapestry he'd better shut up." Moreover, his work so far had been

19   2-2

mainly in one direction—romance. Whether the romance came from the Middle Ages or from that so-called Classical period which is the most romantic of all; whether it had been set in ancient Greece or in uncivilised Europe; whether it had concerned itself with a blood-thirsty legend or the construction of a dining-table of Saxon simplicity, with an effort to rescue the best Norman or Gothic architecture from the hands of the 'restorers,' or the weaving of tapestry beautiful in colour and design—the tendency throughout had been towards romance, particularly the romance of the past. It was evident from the first in *The Defence of Guenevere* as in his one large painting from Malory, and it had run without interruption until 1875. It found perhaps its most definite expression in his home at Kelmscott, where the quiet grey house stood among its water-meadows with nothing more modern than a cart-track to link it to the outside world, and nothing more progressive than Morris himself and his family to show that it belonged to any century later than the sixteenth.

But the year 1876 marks a change, slight but eloquent. With *Sigurd the Volsung* his note changes from the romantic to the epic. The "idle singer of an empty day" has become the solemn prophet, singing of themes that belong to no age but are common to all. The valour of his heroes, who "feared nothing save the loss of honour," their silent smiling resistance of adverse odds, their quiet endurance; and—the other side of the picture—their craft, their lust for revenge, their stark cruelty—all these are part of his picture and are painted in with a high seriousness that he had scarcely achieved before, except possibly here and there in his first volume. Deepest of all is his attitude to death.

> They are gone—the lovely, the mighty, the hope of the ancient Earth,

he wrote of Sigurd and his kin, and this, after doubt and striving, seems to be the quiet result of all his thinking on death, very far removed from the King's reflection in *Atalanta's Race*:

> Lo, I am old, and know what life can be,
> And what a bitter thing is death anear.

In *Love is Enough* we see the poet experimenting, anxious, possibly, to break away from the long line of mere adventure stories, presenting the eternal problems of love in three parallel cases, trying new forms and new metres. It was not a success, but it served its purpose. In *Sigurd* the experiment bears its full fruit. The metre is new to English verse and entirely successful; the story goes grimly on to the grimmest of all possible conclusions—the extinction of all the characters; and the philosophy reaches heights and depths that Morris never again came near.

It would have been impossible, of course, for William Morris to desert romance, and some of the last—and best— of his works were prose romances. But from the days of *Sigurd* a new stage begins in this amazing career. Morris had always laid emphasis in his work on the glory of craftsmanship. In his own sphere the finished article, however it might achieve his aims, would never give quite the same elation as the actual making of it. His letters— particularly at the time when he was learning the dyeing trade—are full of complaints at his lack of time to do everything he could wish; and yet it is easy to read between the lines a boyish enthusiasm for a new hobby. This enthusiasm he tried to instil into others, and in his efforts he discovered what was wrong with English art. The workman, he said, took no interest, no keen personal pride, in the labour of his hands. How could the work of the nineteenth century hope to compare with that of the

Middle Ages when the modern workman treated his job as an unpleasant necessity for a livelihood, whereas the mediaeval workman (said Morris) laboured for love?

The next step was to discover *why* the modern workman lacked the idealism of the mediaeval, and the explanation was found to lie in the conditions of labour, the crude and inartistic surroundings of the poor, the materialism and greed of the rich. To him there became evident an enormous vicious circle. Factories, homes, cities, all were vulgar and inartistic; therefore they produced disgruntled and uninspired workmen, who proceeded to turn out more vulgar and inartistic work. It was not unlike Mr Gordon Bottomley's dreary vision of "machines for making more machines." To cut out the heart of this canker, to change the whole construction of society so that there should no longer be rich or poor, but all happy workmen in different spheres—this became the revolutionary aim for which Morris struggled.

His ideas, of course, were not new. If there had been no other revolutionary prophet, Ruskin would have served for Morris's inspiration. The difference was that Morris spoke with a new and two-fold authority. For he was a workman, as well as a master. He knew the meaning of hard work, as well as the responsibilities and privileges of wealth. A critic once asked him, in fact, why he did not give the millennium a good start by dividing up his own wealth among the poor, and he answered that, while the recipients would get but a few pence each, he himself would lose all the power for the cause that his money gave him. He was not fanatic enough to imagine that he could do everything, but he did what he could, and that was a great deal. In his own factory, though a kind master he was an exacting one, and, while insisting on the quality of the work turned out, endeavoured at the same time to deal generously with all his men. From his own pocket he gave handsomely to the cause, as well as helping deserving cases privately. Of his time and his gifts he was also unstinting, for he (who hated publicity) addressed meetings, wrote pamphlets, 'took the chair,' or stood in wind and rain to answer insolent hecklers or to convert a tiny handful of apathetic loafers. For long periods *The Commonweal*, the organ of the youthful Socialist League, was financed, edited, and almost entirely written by himself alone. In another direction, but for the same cause, was his work on the Society for the Protection of Ancient Buildings, which, together with the Arts and Crafts Exhibition Society, he helped at this time to found. For the former he fought many eager battles in letters to the papers and made many weary journeys in trains (which he hated) and was able successfully to withstand many a movement for disastrous 'restoration.'

All this, of course, told inevitably on his literary work. For years almost the only verse he wrote was political or sociological, almost the only prose, pamphlets or speeches. A great deal of it was very fine and will occupy a prominent place when the full literary history of the Socialist Movement comes to be written. But much of it was written with only half of the great heart and bore all the marks of weariness. For all the while the firm went prosperously on. New premises were taken at Merton Abbey, where the water was most suitable for his dyeing, and at a house on the Thames at Hammersmith (affectionately renamed Kelmscott House), where Morris worked and slept and conducted his business.

Among the partly sociological books of this period were two of his most famous—*A Dream of John Ball* and *News from Nowhere*. The first is a reconstruction of village life in feudal times, with the pleasanter 'Morrisian' features

23

emphasised and the coarser elements mainly ignored. The latter is a fascinating (but unsound) picture of a Utopia based on all Morris's favourite theories Both were enormously popular, and *News from Nowhere*, published in paper covers at a shilling, reached a vast public that scarcely knew anything else of the author.

Within a few years, however, Socialism 'let him down.' It was not that he lost faith in his ideals, or lost hope for the future of the race; but the movement, not yet a 'party,' was young, and like many a young movement contained warring factions. His own wealth and versatility had made him from the first an object of suspicion from his colleagues and of satire from his opponents; there were also anarchist elements with which he could never agree; and finally it was not to be expected that his finer aims would ever secure a large body of support among the working classes. Without regrets then, although with something akin to despair, he withdrew from active political work, although continuing to lend a room at Hammersmith for the meetings of the local League.

Once again comparative leisure bore fruit in literature, and once again it was romance. This time it was prose, and in 1888 he began, significantly at Kelmscott Manor, the last series of his works, including *The House of the Wolfings*, *The Glittering Plain*, and *The Sundering Flood*, the last lines of which were dictated on his death-bed. One more triumph, a part of all his other triumphs, attended his last years—the Kelmscott Press. Just as he had aimed once at producing the perfect home, now he aimed at the perfect book. The type, copied from the best mediaeval Italian and German types, was designed by Morris; some of the vellum came from Rome; Burne-Jones did the principal illustrations, Morris himself the initials and borders. Of the many books produced the most beautiful was the famous Kelmscott Chaucer.

In 1896 he died. Never had one man combined in sixty-two years of life so many purposes, so successfully attained; never did any inventor of stories live so crowded a life himself. In sheer bulk of composition he is almost unrivalled in English Literature; and there is probably none who so consistently reaches a high standard.

It is characteristic of his genius that there is scarcely a line of the many thousands he wrote that stands alone as memorable. In dealing with Rossetti we found the frequent blinding flash that would illumine the page and reveal the genius; with Morris it is otherwise. The light is steady; it seldom sinks; still less frequently does it dazzle. This was strictly in accord with his own ideas of literature. Inspiration he scoffed at; for him genius, if it existed at all, was most certainly a question of taking pains, and everything artistic was a matter of craftsmanship. No trouble was too great; he would rather learn the intricate art of dyeing than put up with the inferior dyes that were sold by the trade, rather learn a difficult new language than suffer a great epic to go unread or untranslated. Although by no means insensitive to the opinions of his friends or of the public he pretended to despise his literary work, or at best to regard it as a relaxation.

His writings offer few problems since they are almost entirely narrative. Nor is there any doubt as to their 'parentage'; the matter is from Froissart, from Malory, from Classical or Norse legend, the manner partly his own, partly from Chaucer—a master to whom he never tired of paying eloquent homage. Much has already been said about their most distinctive feature—their length—and there is little more to add. For Morris contributed little, in the final count, to what he borrowed, and this, more than anything, is what prevents his ranking among our very greatest poets. Some few of the stories may be original, although it is almost as difficult to ascribe a definite origin to them as it is with Shakespeare; but the difference is enormous, for where Shakespeare seized and transfigured a feeble legend Morris would seize and reproduce a noble one.

It is in this reproduction that his greatness lies, for although original creation on the grand scale may be the highest human achievement, the faithful and graphic reconstruction of the past is not far behind. Morris does that; particularly he does it in the vivid sketches of his shorter poems. Often, like Browning's, they have no beginning and no end. The curtain is lifted, as it were, haphazard, and we see into the middle of an event; if we wish to know its causes or its results we must guess. It is like opening a book of very old coloured prints perfectly at random.

To us, after a generation, his position seems secure; among his contemporary critics there were many who doubted. Perhaps his socialistic leanings alienated many who failed to see that they were merely a part of his enthusiasm for the Middle Ages, and who hesitated to prophesy immortality for things with which they disagreed. If we can only approximate to the frame of mind that would hail with joy a new narrative poem from Scott, or, later, a stupendous new 'three-decker' from Lytton, and if, once in that mind, we remember that Morris rarely wished to do more than entertain us—to reconstruct for us the Earthly Paradise—we shall return again and again to the mighty volumes and begin to appreciate, possibly, what this gigantic figure stood for in the prosperous, materialistic days at the end of last century.

These two, then, Morris and Rossetti, represent for us the literary interpretation of that movement in art which was called Pre-Raphaelitism. We have seen its inception, and how rapidly the wave spent itself in pictorial art; and we have seen, now, how much farther it flowed in literature before it lost itself in the empty shallows of 'aestheticism' and 'decadence.' For Rossetti the painting and the writing were things apart; moreover, he seldom either wrote or painted without the white heat of inspiration. For Morris the writing and the designing and the weaving were all one, and for him there was no such thing as inspiration. Therein lies the great gulf between them; but there were other differences. In his poems Rossetti gives us the Middle Ages through the eyes of the painter—the detail, the colour; Morris, though neither vague nor drab, gives us more of the atmosphere, the action, the *dramatis personae*, and what background we find in his work is not usually of his own invention. His is the minstrel's account, rather than the artist's. Other poets there were who gave us mediaeval studies, Swinburne, Browning, Tennyson especially; but none of these approached the intensity of Rossetti (in this particular sphere) or the versatility of Morris. Theirs was a curiously unequal age, when a fierce national self-satisfaction and prosperity went side by side with a keen intellectual activity, when imperialism and jingoism shared the public attention with Omar Khayyam and the Oxford Movement. Perhaps the cult of the mediaeval was the sanest and most sincere of all the contemporary crazes; in any case it could have had no more eloquent prophets than Dante Gabriel Rossetti and William Morris.

DANTE GABRIEL ROSSETTI

The Blessed Damozel

The blessed damozel leaned out
   From the gold bar of Heaven;
Her eyes were deeper than the depth
   Of waters stilled at even;
She had three lilies in her hand,   5
   And the stars in her hair were seven.

Her robe, ungirt from clasp to hem,
   No wrought flowers did adorn,
But a white rose of Mary's gift,
   For service meetly worn;   10
Her hair that lay along her back
   Was yellow like ripe corn.

Herseemed she scarce had been a day
   One of God's choristers;
The wonder was not yet quite gone   15
   From that still look of hers;
Albeit, to them she left, her day
   Had counted as ten years.

(To one, it is ten years of years.
   ...Yet now, and in this place,   20
Surely she leaned o'er me—her hair
   Fell all about my face....
Nothing: the autumn fall of leaves.
   The whole year sets apace.)

It was the rampart of God's house   25
   That she was standing on;
By God built over the sheer depth
   The which is Space begun;
So high, that looking downward thence
   She scarce could see the sun.   30

It lies in Heaven, across the flood
    Of ether, as a bridge.
Beneath, the tides of day and night
    With flame and darkness ridge
The void, as low as where this earth   35
    Spins like a fretful midge.

Heard hardly, some of her new friends
    Amid their loving games
Spake evermore among themselves
    Their virginal chaste names;   40
And the souls mounting up to God
    Went by her like thin flames.

And still she bowed herself and stooped
    Out of the circling charm;
Until her bosom must have made   45
    The bar she leaned on warm,
And the lilies lay as if asleep
    Along her bended arm.

From the fixed place of Heaven she saw
    Time like a pulse shake fierce   50
Through all the worlds. Her gaze still strove
    Within the gulf to pierce
Its path; and now she spoke as when
    The stars sang in their spheres.

The sun was gone now; the curled moon   55
    Was like a little feather
Fluttering far down the gulf; and now
    She spoke through the still weather.
Her voice was like the voice the stars
    Had when they sang together.   60

(Ah sweet! Even now, in that bird's song,
  Strove not her accents there,
Fain to be hearkened? When those bells
  Possessed the mid-day air,
Strove not her steps to reach my side   65
  Down all the echoing stair?)

'I wish that he were come to me,
  For he will come,' she said.
'Have I not prayed in Heaven?—on earth,
  Lord, Lord, has he not pray'd?   70
Are not two prayers a perfect strength?
  And shall I feel afraid?

'When round his head the aureole clings,
  And he is clothed in white,
I'll take his hand and go with him   75
  To the deep wells of light;
We will step down as to a stream,
  And bathe there in God's sight.

'We two will stand beside that shrine,
  Occult, withheld, untrod,   80
Whose lamps are stirred continually
  With prayer sent up to God;
And see our old prayers, granted, melt
  Each like a little cloud.

'We two will lie i' the shadow of   85
  That living mystic tree
Within whose secret growth the Dove
  Is sometimes felt to be,
While every leaf that His plumes touch
  Saith His name audibly.   90

'And I myself will teach to him,
    I myself, lying so,
The songs I sing here; which his voice
    Shall pause in, hushed and slow,
And find some knowledge at each pause,   95
    Or some new thing to know.'

(Alas! We two, we two, thou say'st!
    Yea, one wast thou with me
That once of old. But shall God lift
    To endless unity   100
The soul whose likeness with thy soul
    Was but its love for thee?)

'We two,' she said, 'will seek the groves
    Where the lady Mary is,
With her five handmaidens, whose names   105
    Are five sweet symphonies,
Cecily, Gertrude, Magdalen,
    Margaret and Rosalys.

'Circlewise sit they, with bound locks
    And foreheads garlanded;   110
Into the fine cloth white like flame
    Weaving the golden thread,
To fashion the birth-robes for them
    Who are just born, being dead.

'He shall fear, haply, and be dumb: 115
    Then will I lay my cheek
To his, and tell about our love,
    Not once abashed or weak:
And the dear Mother will approve
    My pride, and let me speak.   120

'Herself shall bring us, hand in hand,
    To Him round whom all souls
Kneel, the clear-ranged unnumbered heads
    Bowed with their aureoles:
And angels meeting us shall sing   125
    To their citherns and citoles.

'There will I ask of Christ the Lord
    Thus much for him and me:—
Only to live as once on earth
    With Love,—only to be,   130
As then awhile, for ever now
    Together, I and he.'

She gazed and listened and then said,
    Less sad of speech than mild,—
'All this is when he comes.' She ceased.   135
    The light thrill'd towards her, fill'd
With angels in strong level flight.
    Her eyes prayed, and she smil'd.

(I saw her smile.) But soon their path
    Was vague in distant spheres: 140
And then she cast her arms along
    The golden barriers,
And laid her face between her hands,
    And wept. (I heard her tears.)

The Staff and Scrip

'Who rules these lands?' the Pilgrim said.
    'Stranger, Queen Blanchelys.'
'And who has thus harried them?' he said.
    'It was Duke Luke did this:
        God's ban be his!'   5

The Pilgrim said: 'Where is your house?
  I'll rest there, with your will.'
'You've but to climb these blackened boughs
  And you'll see it over the hill,
    For it burns still.'   10

'Which road, to seek your Queen?' said he.
  'Nay, nay, but with some wound
You'll fly back hither, it may be,
  And by your blood i' the ground
    My place be found.'   15

'Friend, stay in peace. God keep your head,
  And mine, where I will go;
For He is here and there,' he said.
  He passed the hill-side, slow,
    And stood below.   20

The Queen sat idle by her loom:
  She heard the arras stir,
And looked up sadly: through the room
  The sweetness sickened her
    Of musk and myrrh.   25

Her women, standing two and two,
  In silence combed the fleece.
The Pilgrim said, 'Peace be with you,
  Lady'; and bent his knees.
    She answered, 'Peace.'   30

  Her eyes were like the wave within;
    Like water-reeds the poise
Of her soft body, dainty thin;
    And like the water's noise
      Her plaintive voice.   35

For him, the stream had never well'd
　　In desert tracts malign
So sweet; nor had he ever felt
　　So faint in the sunshine
　　　Of Palestine.　　　　　　　　　40

Right so, he knew that he saw weep
　　Each night through every dream
The Queen's own face, confused in sleep
　　With visages supreme
　　　Not known to him.　　　　　　45

'Lady,' he said, 'your lands lie burnt
　　And waste: to meet your foe
All fear: this I have seen and learnt.
　　Say that it shall be so,
　　　And I will go.'　　　　　　　50

She gazed at him. 'Your cause is just,
　　For I have heard the same':
He said: 'God's strength shall be my trust.
　　Fall it to good or grame,
　　　'Tis in His name.'　　　　　　55

'Sir, you are thanked. My cause is dead.
　　Why should you toil to break
A grave, and fall therein?' she said.
　　He did not pause but spake:
　　　'For my vow's sake.'　　　　　60

　　　*　　　*　　　*　　　*　　　*

They gazed together, he and she,
　　The minute while he spoke;
And when he ceased, she suddenly
　　Looked round upon her folk
　　　As though she woke.　　　　　65

'Fight, Sir,' she said: 'my prayers in pain
  Shall be your fellowship.'
He whispered one among her train,—
  'To-morrow bid her keep
    This staff and scrip.'   70

She sent him a sharp sword, whose belt
  About his body there
As sweet as her own arms he felt.
  He kissed its blade, all bare,
    Instead of her.   75

She sent him a green banner wrought
  With one white lily stem,
To bind his lance with when he fought.
  He writ upon the same
    And kissed her name.   80

She sent him a white shield, whereon
  She bade that he should trace
His will. He blent fair hues that shone,
  And in a golden space
    He kissed her face.   85

Right so, the sunset skies unseal'd,
  Like lands he never knew,
Beyond to-morrow's battle-field
  Lay open out of view
    To ride into.   90

Next day till dark the women pray'd:
  Nor any might know there
How the fight went: the Queen has bade
  That there do come to her
    No messenger.   95

*   *   *   *   *

37

'Oh what is the light that shines so red?
　'Tis long since the sun set';
Quoth the youngest to the eldest maid:
　''Twas dim but now, and yet
　　The light is great.'　　　　　　100

Quoth the other: ''Tis our sight is dazed
　That we see flame i' the air.'
But the Queen held her brows and gazed,
　And said, 'It is the glare
　　Of torches there.'　　　　　　105

'Oh what are the sounds that rise and spread?
　All day it was so still';
Quoth the youngest to the eldest maid;
　'Unto the furthest hill
　　The air they fill.'　　　　　　110

Quoth the other; ''Tis our sense is blurr'd
　With all the chants gone by.'
But the Queen held her breath and heard,
　And said: 'It is the cry
　　Of Victory.'　　　　　　115

The first of all the rout was sound,
　The next were dust and flame,
And then the horses shook the ground:
　And in the thick of them
　　A still band came.　　　　　　120

'Oh what do ye bring out of the fight,
　Thus hid beneath these boughs?'
'Even him, thy conquering guest to-night,
　Who yet shall not carouse,
　　Queen, in thy house.'　　　　　　125

38

'Uncover ye his face,' she said.
  'Oh changed in little space!'
She cried, 'O pale that was so red!
  O God, O God of grace!
    Cover his face.'   130

His sword was broken in his hand
  Where he had kissed the blade.
'O soft steel that could not withstand!
  O my hard heart unstay'd,
    That prayed and prayed.'   135

His bloodied banner crossed his mouth
  Where he had kissed her name.
'O east, and west, and north, and south,
  Fair flew my web, for shame,
    To guide Death's aim!'   140

The tints were shredded from his shield
  Where he had kissed her face.
'Oh, of all gifts that I could yield,
  Death only keeps its place,
    My gift and grace!'   145

Then stepped a damsel to her side,
  And spoke, and needs must weep:
'For his sake, lady, if he died,
  He prayed of thee to keep
    This staff and scrip.'   150

That night they hung above her bed,
  Till morning wet with tears.
Year after year above her head
  Her bed his token wears,
    Five years, ten years.   155

*   *   *   *   *

39

The lists are set in Heaven to-day,
　　The bright pavilions shine;
Fair hangs thy shield, and none gainsay;
　　The trumpets sound in sign
　　　　That she is thine.　　　　　　　160

Not tithed with days' and years' decease
　　He pays thy wage He owed,
But with imperishable peace
　　Here in His own abode,
　　　　Thy jealous God.　　　　　　　165

The Portrait

This is her picture as she was:
　　It seems a thing to wonder on,
As though mine image in the glass
　　Should tarry when myself am gone.
I gaze until she seems to stir,—　　　　5
Until mine eyes almost aver
　　That now, even now, the sweet lips part
　　To breathe the words of the sweet heart:—
And yet the earth is over her.

Alas! even such the thin-drawn ray　　　10
　　That makes the prison-depths more rude,—
The drip of water night and day
　　Giving a tongue to solitude.
Yet this, of all love's perfect prize,
Remains; save what in mournful guise　　15
　　Takes counsel with my soul alone,—
　　Save what is secret and unknown,
Below the earth, above the skies.

In painting her I shrined her face
  Mid mystic trees, where light falls in   20
Hardly at all; a covert place
  Where you might think to find a din
Of doubtful talk, and a live flame
Wandering, and many a shape whose name
  Not itself knoweth, and old dew,   25
  And your own footsteps meeting you,
And all things going as they came.

A deep dim wood; and there she stands
  As in that wood that day: for so
Was the still movement of her hands   30
  And such the pure line's gracious flow.
And passing fair the type must seem,
Unknown the presence and the dream.
  'Tis she: though of herself, alas!
  Less than her shadow on the grass   35
Or than her image in the stream.

That day we met there, I and she
  One with the other all alone;
And we were blithe; yet memory
  Saddens those hours, as when the moon   40
Looks upon daylight. And with her
I stooped to drink the spring-water,
  Athirst where other waters sprang;
  And where the echo is, she sang,—
My soul another echo there.   45

But when that hour my soul won strength
  For words whose silence wastes and kills,
Dull raindrops smote us, and at length
  Thundered the heat within the hills.

That eve I spoke those words again   50
Beside the pelted window-pane;
   And there she hearkened what I said,
   With under-glances that surveyed
The empty pastures blind with rain.

Next day the memories of these things,   55
   Like leaves through which a bird has flown,
Still vibrated with Love's warm wings;
   Till I must make them all my own
And paint this picture. So, 'twixt ease
Of talk and sweet long silences,   60
   She stood among the plants in bloom
   At windows of a summer room,
To feign the shadow of the trees.

And as I wrought, while all above
   And all around was fragrant air,   65
In the sick burthen of my love
   It seemed each sun-thrilled blossom there
Beat like a heart among the leaves.
O heart that never beats nor heaves,
   In that one darkness lying still,   70
   What now to thee my love's great will
Or the fine web the sunshine weaves?

For now doth daylight disavow
   Those days,—nought left to see or hear.
Only in solemn whispers now   75
   At night-time these things reach mine ear,
When the leaf-shadows at a breath
Shrink in the road, and all the heath,
   Forest and water, far and wide,
   In limpid starlight glorified,   80
Lie like the mystery of death.

Last night at last I could have slept,
    And yet delayed my sleep till dawn,
Still wandering. Then it was I wept:
    For unawares I came upon   85
Those glades where once she walked with me:
And as I stood there suddenly,
    All wan with traversing the night,
    Upon the desolate verge of light
Yearned loud the iron-bosomed sea.   90

Even so, where Heaven holds breath and hears
    The beating heart of Love's own breast,—
Where round the secret of all spheres
    All angels lay their wings to rest,—
How shall my soul stand rapt and awed,   95
When, by the new birth borne abroad
    Throughout the music of the suns,
    It enters in her soul at once
And knows the silence there for God!

Here with her face doth memory sit   100
    Meanwhile, and wait the day's decline,
Till other eyes shall look from it,
    Eyes of the spirit's Palestine,
Even than the old gaze tenderer:
While hopes and aims long lost with her   105
    Stand round her image side by side,
    Like tombs of pilgrims that have died
About the Holy Sepulchre.

Sister Helen

'Why did you melt your waxen man,
        Sister Helen?
To-day is the third since you began.'
'The time was long, yet the time ran,
        Little brother.'   5
    (O Mother, Mary Mother,
Three days to-day, between Hell and Heaven!)

'But if you have done your work aright,
        Sister Helen,
You'll let me play, for you said I might.'   10
'Be very still in your play to-night,
        Little brother.'
    (O Mother, Mary Mother,
Third night, to-night, between Hell and Heaven!)

'You said it must melt ere vesper-bell,   15
        Sister Helen;
If now it be molten, all is well.'
'Even so,—nay, peace! you cannot tell,
        Little brother.'
    (O Mother, Mary Mother,   20
O what is this, between Hell and Heaven?)

'Oh the waxen knave was plump to-day,
        Sister Helen;
How like dead folk he has dropped away!'
'Nay now, of the dead what can you say,   25
        Little brother?'
    (O Mother, Mary Mother,
What of the dead, between Hell and Heaven?)

'See, see, the sunken pile of wood,
                    Sister Helen,   30
Shines through the thinned wax red as blood!'
'Nay now, when looked you yet on blood,
                    Little brother?'
            (*O Mother, Mary Mother,*
How pale she is, between Hell and Heaven!)   35

'Now close your eyes, for they're sick and sore,
                    Sister Helen,
And I'll play without the gallery door.'
'Aye, let me rest,—I'll lie on the floor,
                    Little brother.'   40
            (*O Mother, Mary Mother,*
What rest to-night, between Hell and Heaven?)

'Here high up on the balcony,
                    Sister Helen,
The moon flies face to face with me.'   45
'Aye, look and say whatever you see,
                    Little brother.'
            (*O Mother, Mary Mother,*
What sight to-night, between Hell and Heaven?)

'Outside it's merry in the wind's wake,   50
                    Sister Helen;
In the shaken trees the chill stars shake.'
'Hush, heard you a horse-tread as you spake,
                    Little brother?'
            (*O Mother, Mary Mother,*   55
What sound to-night, between Hell and Heaven?)

'I hear a horse-tread, and I see,
                    Sister Helen,
Three horsemen that ride terribly.'

'Little brother, whence come the three,   60
        Little brother?'
      (*O Mother, Mary Mother,*
Whence should they come, between Hell and Heaven?)

'They come by the hill-verge from Boyne Bar,
        Sister Helen,   65
And one draws nigh, but two are afar.'
'Look, look, do you know them who they are,
        Little brother?'
      (*O Mother, Mary Mother,*
Who should they be, between Hell and Heaven?)   70

'Oh, it's Keith of Eastholm rides so fast,
        Sister Helen,
For I know the white mane on the blast.'
'The hour has come, has come at last,
        Little brother!'   75
      (*O Mother, Mary Mother,*
Her hour at last, between Hell and Heaven!)

'He has made a sign and called Halloo!
        Sister Helen,
And he says that he would speak with you.'   80
'Oh tell him I fear the frozen dew,
        Little brother.'
      (*O Mother, Mary Mother,*
Why laughs she thus, between Hell and Heaven?)

'The wind is loud, but I hear him cry,   85
        Sister Helen,
That Keith of Ewern's like to die.'
'And he and thou, and thou and I,
        Little brother.'
      (*O Mother, Mary Mother,*   90
And they and we, between Hell and Heaven!)

'For three days now he has lain abed,
          Sister Helen,
And he prays in torment to be dead.'
'The thing may chance, if he have prayed,   95
          Little brother!'
     (*O Mother, Mary Mother,*
If he have prayed, between Hell and Heaven!)

'But he has not ceased to cry to-day,
          Sister Helen,   100
That you should take your curse away.'
'*My* prayer was heard,—he need but pray,
          Little brother!'
     (*O Mother, Mary Mother,*
Shall God not hear, between Hell and Heaven?) 105

'But he says, till you take back your ban,
          Sister Helen,
His soul would pass, yet never can.'
'Nay then, shall I slay a living man,
          Little brother?'   110
     (*O Mother, Mary Mother,*
A living soul, between Hell and Heaven!)

'But he calls for ever on your name,
          Sister Helen,
And says that he melts before a flame.'   115
'My heart for his pleasure fared the same,
          Little brother.'
     (*O Mother, Mary Mother,*
Fire at the heart, between Hell and Heaven!)

'Here's Keith of Westholm riding fast,   120
          Sister Helen,
For I know the white plume on the blast.'

47

'The hour, the sweet hour I forecast,
        Little brother!'
      (*O Mother, Mary Mother,*   125
Is the hour sweet, between Hell and Heaven?)

'He stops to speak, and he stills his horse,
        Sister Helen;
But his words are drowned in the wind's course.'
'Nay hear, nay hear, you must hear perforce,   130
        Little brother!'
      (*O Mother, Mary Mother,*
A word ill heard, between Hell and Heaven!)

'Oh he says that Keith of Ewern's cry,
        Sister Helen,   135
Is ever to see you ere he die.'
'He sees me in earth, in moon and sky,
        Little brother!'
      (*O Mother, Mary Mother,*
Earth, moon and sky, between Hell and Heaven!) 140

'He sends a ring and a broken coin,
        Sister Helen,
And bids you mind the banks of Boyne.'
'What else he broke will he ever join,
        Little brother?'   145
      (*O Mother, Mary Mother,*
Oh, never more, between Hell and Heaven!)

'He yields you these and craves full fain,
        Sister Helen,
You pardon him in his mortal pain.'   150
'What else he took will he give again,
        Little brother?'
      (*O Mother, Mary Mother,*
No more, no more, between Hell and Heaven!)

'He calls your name in an agony,   155
              Sister Helen,
That even dead Love must weep to see.'
'Hate, born of Love, is blind as he,
              Little brother!'
          (*O Mother, Mary Mother*,   160
Love turned to hate, between Hell and Heaven!)

'Oh it's Keith of Keith now that rides fast,
              Sister Helen,
For I know the white hair on the blast.'
'The short short hour will soon be past,   165
              Little brother!'
          (*O Mother, Mary Mother*,
Will soon be past, between Hell and Heaven!)

'He looks at me and he tries to speak,
              Sister Helen,
But oh! his voice is sad and weak!'   170
'What here should the mighty Baron seek,
              Little brother?'
          (*O Mother, Mary Mother*,
Is this the end, between Hell and Heaven?)   175

'Oh his son still cries, if you forgive,
              Sister Helen,
The body dies but the soul shall live.'
'Fire shall forgive me as I forgive,
              Little brother!'   180
          (*O Mother, Mary Mother*,
As she forgives, between Hell and Heaven!)

'Oh he prays you, as his heart would rive,
              Sister Helen,
To save his dear son's soul alive.'   185

'Nay, flame cannot slay it, it shall thrive,
              Little brother!'
            (*O Mother, Mary Mother,*
Alas, alas, between Hell and Heaven!)

'He cries to you, kneeling in the road,   190
              Sister Helen,
To go with him for the love of God!'
'The way is long to his son's abode,
              Little brother.'
            (*O Mother, Mary Mother,*   195
The way is long, between Hell and Heaven!)

'O Sister Helen, you heard the bell,
              Sister Helen!
More loud than the vesper-chime it fell.'
'No vesper-chime, but a dying knell,   200
              Little brother!'
            (*O Mother, Mary Mother,*
His dying knell, between Hell and Heaven!)

'Alas! but I fear the heavy sound,
              Sister Helen;   205
Is it in the sky or in the ground?'
'Say, have they turned their horses round,
              Little brother?'
            (*O Mother, Mary Mother,*
What would she more, between Hell and Heaven?) 210

'They have raised the old man from his knee,
              Sister Helen,
And they ride in silence hastily.'
'More fast the naked soul doth flee,
              Little brother!'   215
            (*O Mother, Mary Mother,*
The naked soul, between Hell and Heaven!)

'Oh the wind is sad in the iron chill,
             Sister Helen,
And weary sad they look by the hill.'   220
'But Keith of Ewern's sadder still,
             Little brother!'
      (*O Mother, Mary Mother,*
Most sad of all, between Hell and Heaven!)

'See, see, the wax has dropped from its place,   225
             Sister Helen,
And the flames are winning up apace!'
'Yet here they burn but for a space,
             Little brother!'
      (*O Mother, Mary Mother,*   230
Here for a space, between Hell and Heaven!)

'Ah! what white thing at the door has cross'd,
             Sister Helen?
Ah! what is this that sighs in the frost?'
'A soul that's lost as mine is lost,   235
             Little brother!'
      (*O Mother, Mary Mother,*
Lost, lost, all lost, between Hell and Heaven!)

The Stream's Secret

W hat thing unto mine ear
  Wouldst thou convey,—what secret thing,
O wandering water ever whispering?
  Surely thy speech shall be of her.
Thou water, O thou whispering wanderer,   5
  What message dost thou bring?

Say, hath not Love leaned low
This hour beside thy far well-head,
And there through jealous hollowed fingers said
The thing that most I longed to know,—   10
Murmuring with curls all dabbled in thy flow
And washed lips rosy red?

He told it to thee there
Where thy voice hath a louder tone;
But where it welters to this little moan   15
His will decrees that I should hear.
Now speak: for with the silence is no fear,
And I am all alone.

Shall Time not still endow
One hour with life, and I and she   20
Slake in one kiss the thirst of memory?
Say, stream; lest Love should disavow
Thy service, and the bird upon the bough
Sing first to tell it me.

Stream, when this silver thread   25
In flood-time is a torrent brown,
May any bulwark bind thy foaming crown?
Shall not the waters surge and spread
And to the crannied boulders of their bed
Still shoot the dead leaves down?   30

Let no rebuke find place
In speech of thine: or it shall prove
That thou dost ill expound the words of Love,
Even as thine eddy's rippling race
Would blur the perfect image of his face.   35
I will have none thereof.

O learn and understand
That 'gainst the wrongs himself did wreak
Love sought her aid; until her shadowy cheek
    And eyes beseeching gave command;   40
And compassed in her close compassionate hand
    My heart must burn and speak.

    For then at last we spoke
    What eyes so oft had told to eyes
Through that long-lingering silence whose half-sighs 45
    Alone the buried secret broke,
Which with snatched hands and lips' reverberate stroke
    Then from the heart did rise.

    But she is far away
    Now; nor the hours of night grown hoar   50
Bring yet to me, long gazing from the door,
    The wind-stirred robe of roseate grey
And rose-crown of the hour that leads the day
    When we shall meet once more.

    Dark as thy blinded wave   55
    When brimming midnight floods the glen,—
Bright as the laughter of thy runnels when
    The dawn yields all the light they crave;
Even so these hours to wound and that to save
    Are sisters in Love's ken.   60

    Oh sweet her bending grace
    Then when I kneel beside her feet;
And sweet her eyes' o'erhanging heaven; and sweet
    The gathering folds of her embrace;
And her fall'n hair at last shed round my face 65
    When breaths and tears shall meet.

Then by her summoning art
Shall memory conjure back the sere
Autumnal Springs, from many a dying year
   Born dead; and, bitter to the heart,   70
The very ways where now we walk apart
   Who then shall cling so near.

   Pity and love shall burn
In her pressed cheek and cherishing hands;
And from the living spirit of love that stands   75
   Between her lips to soothe and yearn,
Each separate breath shall clasp me round in turn
   And loose my spirit's bands.

   Ah me! with what proud growth
Shall that hour's thirsting race be run;   80
While, for each several sweetness still begun
   Afresh, endures love's endless drouth:
Sweet hands, sweet hair, sweet cheeks, sweet eyes,
      sweet mouth,
   Each singly wooed and won.

   Therefore, when breast and cheek   85
Now part, from long embraces free,—
Each on the other gazing shall but see
   A self that has no need to speak:
All things unsought, yet nothing more to seek,—
   One love in unity.   90

   O water wandering past,—
Albeit to thee I speak this thing,
O water, thou that wanderest whispering,
   Thou keep'st thy counsel to the last.
What spell upon thy bosom should Love cast,   95
   His message thence to wring?

How should all this be told?—
All the sad sum of wayworn days;—
Heart's anguish in the impenetrable maze;
    And on the waste uncoloured wold   100
The visible burthen of the sun grown cold
    And the moon's labouring gaze?

    Stands it not by the door—
Love's Hour—till she and I shall meet;
With bodiless form and unapparent feet   105
    That cast no shadow yet before,
Though round its head the dawn begins to pour
    The breath that makes day sweet?

    Its eyes invisible
Watch till the dial's thin-thrown shade   110
Be born,—yea, till the journeying line be laid
    Upon the point that wakes the spell,
And there in lovelier light than tongue can tell
    Its presence stand array'd.

    But oh! when now her foot   115
Draws near, for whose sake night and day
Were long in weary longing sighed away,—
    The Hour of Love, 'mid airs grown mute,
Shall sing beside the door, and Love's own lute
    Thrill to the passionate lay.   120

    Thou know'st, for Love has told
Within thine ear, O stream, how soon
That song shall lift its sweet appointed tune.
    O tell me, for my lips are cold,
And in my veins the blood is waxing old   125
    Even while I beg the boon.

So, in that hour of sighs
  Assuaged, shall we beside this stone
Yield thanks for grace; while in thy mirror shown
  The twofold image softly lies,   130
Until we kiss, and each in other's eyes
    Is imaged all alone.

  Still silent? Can no art
  Of Love's then move thy pity? Nay,
To thee let nothing come that owns his sway: 135
  Let happy lovers have no part
With thee; nor even so sad and poor a heart
    As thou hast spurned to-day.

  To-day? Lo! night is here.
  The glen grows heavy with some veil   140
Risen from the earth or fall'n to make earth pale;
  And all stands hushed to eye and ear,
Until the night-wind shake the shade like fear
    And every covert quail.

  O soul-sequestered face   145
  Far off,—O were that night but now!
So even beside that stream even I and thou
  Through thirsting lips should draw Love's grace,
And in the zone of that supreme embrace
    Bind aching breast and brow.   150

  O water whispering
  Still through the dark into mine ears,—
As with mine eyes, is it not now with hers?—
  Mine eyes that add to thy cold spring,
Wan water, wandering water weltering,   155
    This hidden tide of tears.

The Card-Dealer

Could you not drink her gaze like wine?
   Yet though its splendour swoon
Into the silence languidly
   As a tune into a tune,
Those eyes unravel the coiled night   5
   And know the stars at noon.

The gold that's heaped beside her hand,
   In truth rich prize it were;
And rich the dreams that wreathe her brows
   With magic stillness there;   10
And he were rich who should unwind
   That woven golden hair.

Around her, where she sits, the dance
   Now breathes its eager heat;
And not more lightly or more true   15
   Fall there the dancers' feet
Than fall her cards on the bright board
   As 'twere an heart that beat.

Her fingers let them softly through,
   Smooth polished silent things;   20
And each one as it falls reflects
   In swift light-shadowings,
Blood-red and purple, green and blue,
   The great eyes of her rings.

Whom plays she with? With thee, who lov'st 25
   Those gems upon her hand;
With me, who search her secret brows;
   With all men, bless'd or bann'd.
We play together, she and we,
   Within a vain strange land: 30

A land without any order,—
  Day even as night, (one saith,)—
Where who lieth down ariseth not
  Nor the sleeper awakeneth;
A land of darkness as darkness itself   35
  And of the shadow of death.

What be her cards, you ask? Even these:—
  The heart, that doth but crave
More, having fed; the diamond,
  Skilled to make base seem brave;   40
The club, for smiting in the dark;
  The spade, to dig a grave.

And do you ask what game she plays?
  With me 'tis lost or won;
With thee it is playing still; with him   45
  It is not well begun;
But 'tis a game she plays with all
  Beneath the sway o' the sun.

Thou seest the card that falls,—she knows
  The card that followeth: 50
Her game in thy tongue is called Life,
  As ebbs thy daily breath:
When she shall speak, thou'lt learn her tongue
  And know she calls it Death.

The Ballad of Dead Ladies

Tell me now in what hidden way is
  Lady Flora, the lovely Roman?
Where's Hipparchia, and where is Thaïs,
  Neither of them the fairer woman?

Where is Echo, beheld of no man,　　　　5
Only heard on river and mere,—
　　She whose beauty was more than human?...
But where are the snows of yester-year?

Where's Héloïse, the learned nun,
　　For whose sake Abeillard, I ween,　　　10
Lost manhood and put priesthood on?
　　(From Love he won such dule and teen!)
　　And where, I pray you, is the Queen
Who willed that Buridan should steer
　　Sewed in a sack's mouth down the Seine?... 15
But where are the snows of yester-year?

White Queen Blanche, like a queen of lilies,
　　With a voice like any mermaiden—
Bertha Broadfoot, Beatrice, Alice,
　　And Ermengarde the lady of Maine,—　　20
　　And that good Joan whom Englishmen
At Rouen doomed and burned her there,—
　　Mother of God, where are they then?...
But where are the snows of yester-year?

Nay, never ask this week, fair lord,　　　25
　　Where they are gone, nor yet this year,
Except with this for an overword,—
　　But where are the snows of yester-year?

My Father's Close

(Old French)

Inside my father's close,
   (Fly away O my heart away!)
Sweet apple-blossom blows
     So sweet.

Three kings' daughters fair,   5
   (Fly away O my heart away!)
They lie below it there
     So sweet.

'Ah!' says the eldest one,
   (Fly away O my heart away!)   10
'I think the day's begun
     So sweet.'

'Ah!' says the second one,
   (Fly away O my heart away!)
'Far off I hear the drum   15
     So sweet.'

'Ah!' says the youngest one,
   (Fly away O my heart away!)
'It's my true love, my own,
     So sweet.   20

'Oh! if he fight and win,'
   (Fly away O my heart away!)
'I keep my love for him,
     So sweet:
'Oh! let him lose or win,   25
     He hath it still complete.'

The Birth Bond

Have you not noted, in some family
    Where two were born of a first marriage-bed,
    How still they own their gracious bond, though fed
And nursed on the forgotten breast and knee?
How to their father's children they shall be   5
    In act and thought of one goodwill; but each
    Shall for the other have, in silence speech,
And in a word complete community?

Even so, when first I saw you, seemed it, love,
    That among souls allied to mine was yet   10
One nearer kindred than life hinted of.
    O born with me somewhere that men forget,
    And though in years of sight and sound unmet,
Known for my soul's birth-partner well enough!

Lost Days

The lost days of my life until to-day,
    What were they, could I see them on the street
    Lie as they fell? Would they be ears of wheat
Sown once for food but trodden into clay?
Or golden coins squandered and still to pay?   5
    Or drops of blood dabbling the guilty feet?
    Or such spilt water as in dreams must cheat
The throats of men in Hell, who thirst alway?

I do not see them here; but after death
    God knows I know the faces I shall see,   10
Each one a murdered self, with low last breath.
    'I am thyself,—what hast thou done to me?'
    'And I—and I—thyself,' (lo! each one saith,)
'And thou thyself to all eternity!'

A Superscription

Look in my face; my name is Might-have-been;
  I am also called No-more, Too-late, Farewell;
  Unto thine ear I hold the dead-sea shell
Cast up thy Life's foam-fretted feet between;
Unto thine eyes the glass where that is seen   5
  Which had Life's form and Love's, but by my spell
  Is now a shaken shadow intolerable,
Of ultimate things unuttered the frail screen.

Mark me, how still I am! But should there dart
  One moment through thy soul the soft surprise   10
  Of that winged Peace which lulls the breath of sighs,—
Then shalt thou see me smile, and turn apart
Thy visage to mine ambush at thy heart,
  Sleepless with cold commemorative eyes.

Newborn Death

I

To-day Death seems to me an infant child
  Which her worn mother Life upon my knee
  Has set to grow my friend and play with me;
If haply so my heart might be beguil'd
To find no terrors in a face so mild,—   5
  If haply so my weary heart might be
  Unto the newborn milky eyes of thee,
O Death, before resentment reconcil'd.

How long, O Death? And shall thy feet depart
  Still a young child's with mine, or wilt thou stand 10
Fullgrown the helpful daughter of my heart,
  What time with thee indeed I reach the strand
Of the pale wave which knows thee what thou art,
  And drink it in the hollow of thy hand?

And thou, O Life, the lady of all bliss,   15
  With whom, when our first heart beat full and fast,
  I wandered till the haunts of men were pass'd,
And in fair places found all bowers amiss
Till only woods and waves might hear our kiss,
  While to the winds all thought of Death we cast:— 20
  Ah, Life! and must I have from thee at last
No smile to greet me and no babe but this?

Lo! Love, the child once ours; and Song, whose hair
  Blew like a flame and blossomed like a wreath;
And Art, whose eyes were worlds by God found fair; 25
  These o'er the book of Nature mixed their breath
With neck-twined arms, as oft we watched them there:
  And did these die that thou mightst bear me Death?

Love-lily

Between the hands, between the brows,
  Between the lips of Love-lily,
A spirit is born whose birth endows
  My blood with fire to burn through me;
Who breathes upon my gazing eyes,   5
  Who laughs and murmurs in mine ear,
At whose least touch my colour flies,
  And whom my life grows faint to hear.

Within the voice, within the heart,
  Within the mind of Love-lily,   10
A spirit is born who lifts apart
  His tremulous wings and looks at me;
Who on my mouth his finger lays,
  And shows, while whispering lutes confer,
That Eden of Love's watered ways   15
  Whose winds and spirits worship her.

Brows, hands, and lips, heart, mind, and voice,
　　Kisses and words of Love-lily,—
Oh! bid me with your joy rejoice
　　Till riotous longing rest in me!　　20
Ah! let no hope be still distraught,
　　But find in her its gracious goal,
Whose speech Truth knows not from her thought
　　Nor Love her body from her soul.

Sudden Light

I have been here before,
　　But when or how I cannot tell:
I know the grass beyond the door,
　　The sweet keen smell,
The sighing sound, the lights around the shore.　　5

You have been mine before,—
　　How long ago I may not know:
But just when at that swallow's soar
　　Your neck turned so,
Some veil did fall,—I knew it all of yore.　　10

Then, now,—perchance again!...
　　O round mine eyes your tresses shake!
Shall we not lie as we have lain
　　Thus for Love's sake,
And sleep, and wake, yet never break the chain?　　15

The Woodspurge

The wind flapped loose, the wind was still,
Shaken out dead from tree and hill:
I had walked on at the wind's will,—
I sat now, for the wind was still.

Between my knees my forehead was,— 5
My lips, drawn in, said not Alas!
My hair was over in the grass,
My naked ears heard the day pass.

My eyes, wide open, had the run
Of some ten weeds to fix upon; 10
Among those few, out of the sun,
The woodspurge flowered, three cups in one.

From perfect grief there need not be
Wisdom or even memory:
One thing then learnt remains to me,— 15
The woodspurge has a cup of three.

Mary's Girlhood

(For a picture)

This is that blessed Mary, pre-elect
  God's Virgin. Gone is a great while, and she
  Dwelt young in Nazareth of Galilee.
Unto God's will she brought devout respect,
Profound simplicity of intellect, 5
  And supreme patience. From her mother's knee
  Faithful and hopeful; wise in charity;
Strong in grave peace; in pity circumspect.

So held she through her girlhood; as it were
  An angel-watered lily, that near God 10
    Grows and is quiet. Till, one dawn at home,
She woke in her white bed, and had no fear
  At all,—yet wept till sunshine, and felt awed:
    Because the fulness of the time was come.

Down Stream

Between Holmscote and Hurstcote
    The river-reaches wind,
The whispering trees accept the breeze,
    The ripple's cool and kind:
With love low-whispered 'twixt the shores,   5
    With rippling laughters gay,
With white arms bared to ply the oars,
    On last year's first of May.

Between Holmscote and Hurstcote
    The river's brimmed with rain,   10
Through close-met banks and parted banks
    Now near, now far again:
With parting tears caressed to smiles,
    With meeting promised soon,
With every sweet vow that beguiles,   15
    On last year's first of June.

Between Holmscote and Hurstcote
    The river's flecked with foam,
'Neath shuddering clouds that hang in shrouds
    And lost winds wild for home: 20
With infant wailings at the breast,
    With homeless steps astray,
With wanderings shuddering tow'rds one rest
    On this year's first of May.

Between Holmscote and Hurstcote   25
    The summer river flows
With doubled flight of moons by night
    And lilies' deep repose:

With lo! beneath the moon's white stare
    A white face not the moon,   30
With lilies meshed in tangled hair,
    On this year's first of June.

Between Holmscote and Hurstcote
    A troth was given and riven,
From heart's trust grew one life to two,   35
    Two lost lives cry to Heaven:
With banks spread calm to meet the sky,
    With meadows newly mowed,
The harvest-paths of glad July,
    The sweet school-children's road.   40

The White Ship

(HENRY I OF ENGLAND—25th November, 1120)

By none but me can the tale be told,
The butcher of Rouen, poor Berold.
    (*Lands are swayed by a King on a throne.*)

'Twas a royal train put forth to sea,
Yet the tale can be told by none but me.   5
    (*The sea hath no King but God alone.*)

King Henry held it as life's whole gain
That after his death his son should reign.

'Twas so in my youth I heard men say,
And my old age calls it back to-day.   10

King Henry of England's realm was he,
And Henry Duke of Normandy.

The times had changed when on either coast
'Clerkly Harry' was all his boast.

67

Of ruthless strokes full many an one   15
He had struck to crown himself and his son;
And his elder brother's eyes were gone.

And when to the chase his court would crowd,
The poor flung ploughshares on his road,
And shrieked: 'Our cry is from King to God!'   20

But all the chiefs of the English land
Had knelt and kissed the Prince's hand.

And next with his son he sailed to France
To claim the Norman allegiance:

And every baron in Normandy   25
Had taken the oath of fealty.

'Twas sworn and sealed, and the day had come
When the King and the Prince might journey home:

For Christmas cheer is to home hearts dear,
And Christmas now was drawing near.   30

Stout Fitz-Stephen came to the King,—
A pilot famous in seafaring;

And he held to the King, in all men's sight,
A mark of gold for his tribute's right.

'Liege Lord! my father guided the ship   35
From whose boat your father's foot did slip
When he caught the English soil in his grip,

'And cried: "By this clasp I claim command
O'er every rood of English land!"

'He was borne to the realm you rule o'er now   40
In that ship with the archer carved at her prow:

'And thither I'll bear, an it be my due,
Your father's son and his grandson too.

68

'The famed White Ship is mine in the bay,
From Harfleur's harbour she sails to-day,   45

'With masts fair-pennoned as Norman spears
And with fifty well-tried mariners.'

Quoth the King: 'My ships are chosen each one,
But I'll not say nay to Stephen's son.

'My son and daughter and fellowship   50
Shall cross the water in the White Ship.'

The King set sail with the eve's south wind,
And soon he left that coast behind.

The Prince and all his, a princely show,
Remained in the good White Ship to go.   55

With noble knights and with ladies fair,
With courtiers and sailors gathered there,
Three hundred living souls we were:

And I, Berold, was the meanest hind
In all that train to the Prince assign'd.   60

The Prince was a lawless shameless youth;
From his father's loins he sprang without ruth:

Eighteen years till then he had seen,
And the devil's dues in him were eighteen.

And now he cried: 'Bring wine from below;   65
Let the sailors revel ere yet they row:

'Our speed shall o'ertake my father's flight
Though we sail from the harbour at midnight.'

The rowers made good cheer without check;
The lords and ladies obeyed his beck;   70
The night was light, and they danced on the deck.

But at midnight's stroke they cleared the bay,
And the White Ship furrowed the water-way.

The sails were set, and the oars kept tune
To the double flight of the ship and the moon: 75

Swifter and swifter the White Ship sped
Till she flew as the spirit flies from the dead:

As white as a lily glimmered she
Like a ship's fair ghost upon the sea.

And the Prince cried, 'Friends, 'tis the hour to sing! 80
Is a songbird's course so swift on the wing?'

And under the winter stars' still throng,
From brown throats, white throats, merry and strong,
The knights and the ladies raised a song.

A song,—nay, a shriek that rent the sky,   85
That leaped o'er the deep!—the grievous cry
Of three hundred living that now must die.

An instant shriek that sprang to the shock
As the ship's keel felt the sunken rock.

'Tis said that afar—a shrill strange sigh—   90
The King's ships heard it and knew not why.

Pale Fitz-Stephen stood by the helm
'Mid all those folk that the waves must whelm.

A great King's heir for the waves to whelm,
And the helpless pilot pale at the helm!   95

The ship was eager and sucked athirst,
By the stealthy stab of the sharp reef pierc'd:

And like the moil round a sinking cup,
The waters against her crowded up.

A moment the pilot's senses spin,— 100
The next he snatched the Prince 'mid the din,
Cut the boat loose, and the youth leaped in.

A few friends leaped with him, standing near.
'Row! the sea's smooth and the night is clear!'

'What! none to be saved but these and I?' 105
'Row, row as you'd live! All here must die!'

Out of the churn of the choking ship,
Which the gulf grapples and the waves strip,
They struck with the strained oars' flash and dip.

'Twas then o'er the splitting bulwarks' brim 110
The Prince's sister screamed to him.

He gazed aloft, still rowing apace,
And through the whirled surf he knew her face.

To the toppling decks clave one and all
As a fly cleaves to a chamber-wall. 115

I, Berold, was clinging anear;
I prayed for myself and quaked with fear,
But I saw his eyes as he looked at her.

He knew her face and he heard her cry,
And he said, 'Put back! she must not die!' 120

And back with the current's force they reel
Like a leaf that's drawn to a water-wheel.

'Neath the ship's travail they scarce might float,
But he rose and stood in the rocking boat.

Low the poor ship leaned on the tide: 125
O'er the naked keel as she best might slide,
The sister toiled to the brother's side.

He reached an oar to her from below,
And stiffened his arms to clutch her so.

But now from the ship some spied the boat,   130
And 'Saved!' was the cry from many a throat.

And down to the boat they leaped and fell:
It turned as a bucket turns in a well,
And nothing was there but the surge and swell.

The Prince that was and the King to come,   135
There in an instant gone to his doom,

Despite of all England's bended knee
And maugre the Norman fealty!

He was a Prince of lust and pride;
He showed no grace till the hour he died.   140

When he should be King, he oft would vow,
He'd yoke the peasant to his own plough.
O'er him the ships score their furrows now.

God only knows where his soul did wake,
But I saw him die for his sister's sake.   145

By none but me can the tale be told,
The butcher of Rouen, poor Berold.
   (*Lands are swayed by a King on a throne.*)

'Twas a royal train put forth to sea,
Yet the tale can be told by none but me.   150
   (*The sea hath no King but God alone.*)

*   *   *   *   *

And when I rose, 'twas the sea did seem,
And not these things, to be all a dream.

The ship was gone and the crowd was gone,
And the deep shuddered and the moon shone,   155

And in a strait grasp my arms did span
The mainyard rent from the mast where it ran;
And on it with me was another man.

Where lands were none 'neath the dim sea-sky,
We told our names, that man and I.   160

'O I am Godefroy de l'Aigle hight,
And son I am to a belted knight.'

'And I am Berold the butcher's son
Who slays the beasts in Rouen town.'

Then cried we upon God's name, as we   165
Did drift on the bitter winter sea.

But lo! a third man rose o'er the wave,
And we said, 'Thank God! us three may He save!'

He clutched to the yard with panting stare,
And we looked and knew Fitz-Stephen there.   170

He clung, and 'What of the Prince?' quoth he.
'Lost, lost!' we cried. He cried, 'Woe on me!'
And loosed his hold and sank through the sea.

And soul with soul again in that space
We two were together face to face: 175

And each knew each, as the moments sped,
Less for one living than for one dead:

And every still star overhead
Seemed an eye that knew we were but dead.

And the hours passed; till the noble's son   180
Sighed, 'God be thy help! my strength's foredone!

'O farewell, friend, for I can no more!'
'Christ take thee!' I moaned; and his life was o'er.

73

Three hundred souls were all lost but one,
And I drifted over the sea alone. 185

At last the morning rose on the sea
Like an angel's wing that beat tow'rds me.

Sore numbed I was in my sheepskin coat;
Half dead I hung, and might nothing note,
Till I woke sun-warmed in a fisher-boat. 190

The sun was high o'er the eastern brim
As I praised God and gave thanks to Him.

That day I told my tale to a priest,
Who charged me, till the shrift were releas'd,
That I should keep it in mine own breast. 195

And with the priest I thence did fare
To King Henry's court at Winchester.

We spoke with the King's high chamberlain,
And he wept and mourned again and again,
As if his own son had been slain: 200

And round us ever there crowded fast
Great men with faces all aghast:

And who so bold that might tell the thing
Which now they knew to their lord the King?
Much woe I learnt in their communing. 205

The King had watched with a heart sore stirred
For two whole days, and this was the third:

*   *   *   *   *

But who should speak to-day of the thing
That all knew there except the King?

Then pondering much they found a way, 210
And met round the King's high seat that day:

74

And the King sat with a heart sore stirred,
And seldom he spoke and seldom heard.

'Twas then through the hall the King was 'ware
Of a little boy with golden hair, 215

As bright as the golden poppy is
That the beach breeds for the surf to kiss:

Yet pale his cheek as the thorn in Spring,
And his garb black like the raven's wing.

Nothing heard but his foot through the hall, 220
For now the lords were silent all.

And the King wondered, and said, 'Alack!
Who sends me a fair boy dressed in black?

'Why, sweet heart, do you pace through the hall
As though my court were a funeral?' 225

Then lowly knelt the child at the dais,
And looked up weeping in the King's face.

'O wherefore black, O King, ye may say,
For white is the hue of death to-day.

'Your son and all his fellowship 230
Lie low in the sea with the White Ship.'

King Henry fell as a man struck dead;
And speechless still he stared from his bed
When to him next day my rede I read.

There's many an hour must needs beguile 235
A King's high heart that he should smile,—

Full many a lordly hour, full fain
Of his realm's rule and pride of his reign:—

But this King never smiled again.

75

By none but me can the tale be told, 240
The butcher of Rouen, poor Berold.
  (*Lands are swayed by a King on a throne.*)

'Twas a royal train put forth to sea,
But the tale can be told by none but me.
  (*The sea hath no King but God alone.*) 245

Soothsay

Let no man ask thee of anything
Not yearborn between Spring and Spring.
More of all worlds than he can know,
Each day the single sun doth show.
A trustier gloss than thou canst give 5
From all wise scrolls demonstrative,
The sea doth sigh and the wind sing.

Let no man awe thee on any height
Of earthly kingship's mouldering might.
The dust his heel holds meet for thy brow 10
Hath all of it been what both are now;
And thou and he may plague together
A beggar's eyes in some dusty weather
When none that is now knows sound or sight.

Crave thou no dower of earthly things 15
Unworthy Hope's imaginings.
To have brought true birth of Song to be
And to have won hearts to Poesy,
Or anywhere in the sun or rain
To have loved and been beloved again, 20
Is loftiest reach of Hope's bright wings.

The wild waifs cast up by the sea
Are diverse ever seasonably.

76

Even so the soul-tides still may land
A different drift upon the sand.　　　　25
But one the sea is evermore:
And one be still, 'twixt shore and shore,
As the sea's life, thy soul in thee.

Say, hast thou pride? How then may fit
Thy mood with flatterers' silk-spun wit?　　30
Haply the sweet voice lifts thy crest,
A breeze of fame made manifest.
Nay, but then chaf'st at flattery? Pause:
Be sure thy wrath is not because
It makes thee feel thou lovest it.　　　35

Let thy soul strive that still the same
Be early friendship's sacred flame.
The affinities have strongest part
In youth, and draw men heart to heart:
As life wears on and finds no rest,　　40
The individual in each breast
Is tyrannous to sunder them.

In the life-drama's stern cue-call,
A friend's a part well-prized by all:
And if thou meet an enemy,　　　　45
What art thou that none such should be?
Even so: but if the two parts run
Into each other and grow one,
Then comes the curtain's cue to fall.

Whate'er by other's need is claimed　　50
More than by thine,—to him unblamed
Resign it: and if he should hold
What more than he thou lack'st, bread, gold,
Or any good whereby we live,—
To thee such substance let him give　　55
Freely: nor he nor thou be shamed.

77

Strive that thy works prove equal: lest
That work which thou hast done the best
Should come to be to thee at length
(Even as to envy seems the strength   60
Of others) hateful and abhorr'd,—
Thine own above thyself made lord,—
Of self-rebuke the bitterest.

Unto the man of yearning thought
And aspiration, to do nought   65
Is in itself almost an act,—
Being chasm-fire and cataract
Of the soul's utter depths unseal'd.
Yet woe to thee if once thou yield
Unto the act of doing nought!   70

How callous seems beyond revoke
The clock with its last listless stroke!
How much too late at length!—to trace
The hour on its forewarning face,
The thing thou hast not dared to do!...   75
Behold, this *may* be thus! Ere true
It prove, arise and bear thy yoke.

Let lore of all Theology
Be to thy soul what it *can* be:
But know,—the Power that fashions man   80
Measured not out thy little span
For thee to take the meting-rod
In turn, and so approve on God
Thy science of Theometry.

To God at best, to Chance at worst,   85
Give thanks for good things, last as first.
But windstrown blossom is that good
Whose apple is not gratitude.

Even if no prayer uplift thy face,
Let the sweet right to render grace 90
As thy soul's cherished child be nurs'd.

Didst ever say, 'Lo, I forget'?
Such thought was to remember yet.
As in a gravegarth, count to see
The monuments of memory. 95
Be this thy soul's appointed scope:—
Gaze onward without claim to hope,
Nor, gazing backward, court regret.

The Cloud Confines

The day is dark and the night
    To him that would search their heart;
    No lips of cloud that will part
Nor morning song in the light:
    Only, gazing alone, 5
    To him wild shadows are shown,
    Deep under deep unknown
And height above unknown height.
        Still we say as we go,—
            'Strange to think by the way, 10
            Whatever there is to know,
                That shall we know one day.'

The Past is over and fled;
    Named new, we name it the old;
    Thereof some tale hath been told, 15
But no word comes from the dead;
    Whether at all they be,
    Or whether as bond or free,
    Or whether they too were we,
Or by what spell they have sped. 20

79

Still we say as we go,—
'Strange to think by the way,
Whatever there is to know,
That shall we know one day.'

What of the heart of hate   25
That beats in thy breast, O Time?—
Red strife from the furthest prime,
And anguish of fierce debate;
War that shatters her slain,
And peace that grinds them as grain,   30
And eyes fixed ever in vain
On the pitiless eyes of Fate.
Still we say as we go,—
'Strange to think by the way,
Whatever there is to know,   35
That shall we know one day.'

What of the heart of love
That bleeds in thy breast, O Man?—
Thy kisses snatched 'neath the ban
Of fangs that mock them above;   40
Thy bells prolonged unto knells,
Thy hope that a breath dispels,
Thy bitter forlorn farewells
And the empty echoes thereof?
Still we say as we go,—   45
'Strange to think by the way,
Whatever there is to know,
That shall we know one day.'

The sky leans dumb on the sea,
Aweary with all its wings;   50
And oh! the song the sea sings
Is dark everlastingly.

Our past is clean forgot,
Our present is and is not,
Our future's a sealed seedplot,   55
And what betwixt them are we?—
    We who say as we go,—
        'Strange to think by the way,
    Whatever there is to know,
        That shall we know one day   60

Winter

How large that thrush looks on the bare thorn-tree!
  A swarm of such, three little months ago,
  Had hidden in the leaves and let none know
Save by the outburst of their minstrelsy.
A white flake here and there—a snow lily   5
  Of last night's frost—our naked flower-beds hold;
  And for a rose-flower on the darkling mould
The hungry redbreast gleams. No bloom, no bee.

The current shudders to its ice-bound sedge:
  Nipped in their bath, the stark reeds one by one   10
  Flash each its clinging diamond in the sun:
'Neath winds which for this winter's sovereign pledge
Shall curb great king-masts to the ocean's edge
  And leave memorial forest-kings o'erthrown.

Spring

Soft-littered is the new-year's lambing-fold,
  And in the hollowed haystack at its side
  The shepherd lies o' nights now, wakeful-eyed
At the ewes' travailing call through the dark cold.

The young rooks cheep 'mid the thick caw o' the old: 5
And near unpeopled stream-sides, on the ground,
By her Spring cry the moorhen's nest is found,
Where the drained flood-lands flaunt their marigold.

Chill are the gusts to which the pastures cower,
And chill the current where the young reeds stand 10
As green and close as the young wheat on land:
Yet here the cuckoo and the cuckoo-flower
Plight to the heart Spring's perfect imminent hour
Whose breath shall soothe you like your dear one's hand.

From Hand and Soul

Chiaro was now famous. It was for the race of fame
that he had girded up his loins; and he had not paused until
fame was reached; yet now, in taking breath, he found
that the weight was still at his heart. The years of his labour
had fallen from him, and his life was still in its first painful 5
desire.

With all that Chiaro had done during these three years,
and even before, with the studies of his early youth, there
had always been a feeling of worship and service. It was
the peace-offering that he made to God and to his own 10
soul for the eager selfishness of his aim. There was earth,
indeed, upon the hem of his raiment; but *this* was of the
heaven, heavenly He had seasons when he could endure
to think of no other feature of his hope than this: and some-
times, in the ecstasy of prayer, it had even seemed to him to 15
behold that day when his mistress—his mystical lady (now
hardly in her ninth year, but whose smile at meeting had
already lighted on his soul)—even she, his own gracious
Italian Art—should pass, through the sun that never sets,
into the shadow of the tree of life, and be seen of God, and 20
found good: and then it had seemed to him that he,

with many who, since his coming, had joined the band of whom he was one (for, in his dream, the body he had worn on earth had been dead an hundred years), were permitted to gather round the blessed maiden, and to 25 worship with her through all ages and ages of ages, saying, Holy, holy, holy. This thing he had seen with the eyes of his spirit; and in this thing had trusted, believing that it would surely come to pass.

But now (being at length led to inquire closely into 30 himself), even as, in the pursuit of fame, the unrest abiding after attainment had proved to him that he had misinterpreted the craving of his own spirit—so also, now that he would willingly have fallen back on devotion, he became aware that much of that reverence which he had mistaken 35 for faith had been no more than the worship of beauty. Therefore, after certain days passed in perplexity, Chiaro said within himself, 'My life and my will are yet before me: I will take another aim to my life.'

From that moment Chiaro set a watch on his soul, and 40 put his hand to no other works but only to such as had for their end the presentment of some moral greatness that should influence the beholder: and, to this end, he multiplied abstractions, and forgot the beauty and passion of the world. So the people ceased to throng about his pictures 45 as heretofore; and, when they were carried through town and town to their destination, they were no longer delayed by the crowds eager to gaze and admire; and no prayers or offerings were brought to them on their path, as to his Madonnas, and his Saints, and his Holy Children, 50 wrought for the sake of the life he saw in the faces that he loved. Only the critical audience remained to him; and these, in default of more worthy matter, would have turned their scrutiny on a puppet or a mantle. Meanwhile, he had no more of fever upon him; but was calm and 55 pale each day in all that he did and in his goings in and out. The works he produced at this time have perished— in all likelihood, not unjustly. It is said (and we may easily believe it), that, though more laboured than his former pictures, they were cold and unemphatic; bearing marked 60 out upon them the measure of that boundary to which they were made to conform.

And the weight was still close at Chiaro's heart: but he held in his breath, never resting (for he was afraid), and would not know it. 65

*   *   *   *   *

Chiaro sat with his face in his open hands. Once again he had wished to set his foot on a place that looked green and fertile; and once again it seemed to him that the thin rank mask was about to spread away, and that this time the chill of the water must leave leprosy in his flesh. The 70 light still swam in his head, and bewildered him at first; but when he knew his thoughts, they were these:—

'Fame failed me: faith failed me: and now this also,— the hope that I nourished in this my generation of men,— shall pass from me, and leave my feet and my hands groping. 75 Yet because of this are my feet become slow and my hands thin. I am as one who, through the whole night, holding his way diligently, hath smitten the steel unto the flint, to lead some whom he knew darkling; who hath kept his eyes always on the sparks that himself made, lest they 80 should fail; and who, towards dawn, turning to bid them that he had guided God speed, sees the wet grass untrodden except of his own feet. I am as the last hour of the day, whose chimes are a perfect number; whom the next followeth not, nor light ensueth from him; but 85 in the same darkness is the old order begun afresh. Men say, "This is not God nor man; he is not as we are, neither above us: let him sit beneath us, for we are many." Where

84

I write Peace, in that spot is the drawing of swords, and there men's footprints are red. When I would sow, an- other harvest is ripe. Nay, it is much worse with me than thus much. Am I not as a cloth drawn before the light, that the looker may not be blinded? but which showeth thereby the grain of its own coarseness, so that the light seems defiled, and men say, "We will not walk by it." Wherefore through me they shall be doubly accursed, seeing that through me they reject the light. May one be a devil and not know it?'

As Chiaro was in these thoughts, the fever encroached slowly on his veins, till he could sit no longer and would have risen; but suddenly he found awe within him, and held his head bowed, without stirring. The warmth of the air was not shaken; but there seemed a pulse in the light, and a living freshness, like rain. The silence was a painful music, that made the blood ache in his temples; and he lifted his face and his deep eyes.

A woman was present in his room, clad to the hands and feet with a green and grey raiment, fashioned to that time. It seemed that the first thoughts he had ever known were given him as at first from her eyes, and he knew her hair to be the golden veil through which he beheld his dreams. Though her hands were joined, her face was not lifted, but set forward; and though the gaze was austere, yet her mouth was supreme in gentleness. And as he looked, Chiaro's spirit appeared abashed of its own intimate presence, and his lips shook with the thrill of tears; it seemed such a bitter while till the spirit might be indeed alone.

She did not move closer towards him, but he felt her to be as much with him as his breath. He was like one who, scaling a great steepness, hears his own voice echoed in some place much higher than he can see, and the name of which is not known to him. As the woman stood, her speech was with Chiaro: not, as it were, from her mouth or in his ears; but distinctly between them.   125

'I am an image, Chiaro, of thine own soul within thee. See me, and know me as I am. Thou sayest that fame has failed thee, and faith failed thee; but because at least thou hast not laid thy life unto riches, therefore, though thus late, I am suffered to come into thy knowledge. Fame 130 sufficed not, for that thou didst seek fame: seek thine own conscience (not thy mind's conscience, but thine heart's), and all shall approve and suffice. For Fame, in noble soils, is a fruit of the Spring: but not therefore should it be said: "Lo! my garden that I planted is barren: the crocus is 135 here, but the lily is dead in the dry ground, and shall not lift the earth that covers it: therefore I will fling my garden together, and give it unto the builders." Take heed rather that thou trouble not the wise secret earth; for in the mould that thou throwest up shall the first tender growth 140 lie to waste; which else had been strong in its season. Yea, and even if the year fall past in all its months, and the soil be indeed, to thee, peevish and incapable, and though thou indeed gather all thy harvest, and it suffice for others, and thou remain vext with emptiness; and 145 others drink of thy streams, and the drouth rasp thy throat;—let it be enough that these have found the feast good, and thanked the giver: remembering that, when the winter is striven through, there is another year, whose wind is meek, and whose sun fulfilleth all....   150

'Chiaro, servant of God, take now thine Art unto thee, and paint me thus, as I am, to know me: weak, as I am, and in the weeds of this time; only with eyes which seek out labour, and with a faith, not learned, yet jealous of prayer. Do this; so shall thy soul stand before thee always, 155 and perplex thee no more.'

And Chiaro did as she bade him. While he worked, his face grew solemn with knowledge : and before the shadows had turned, his work was done. Having finished, he lay back where he sat, and was asleep immediately; for the 160 growth of that strong sunset was heavy about him, and he felt weak and haggard; like one just come out of a dusk, hollow country, bewildered with echoes, where he had lost himself, and who has not slept for many days and nights. And when she saw him lie back, the beautiful woman came 165 to him, and sat at his head, gazing, and quieted his sleep with her voice....

WILLIAM MORRIS

From Frank's Sealed Letter

Ever since I can remember, even when I was quite a child, people have always told me that I had no perseverance, no strength of will; they have always kept on saying to me, directly and indirectly, 'Unstable as water thou shalt not excel'; and they have always been quite wrong in this 5 matter, for of all men I ever heard of, I have the strongest will for good and evil. I could soon find out whether a thing were possible or not to me; then if it were not, I threw it away for ever, never thought of it again, no regret, no longing for that, it was past, and over to me; but if it 10 were possible, and I made up my mind to do it, then and there I began it, and in due time finished it, turning neither to the right hand nor the left, till it was done. So I did with all things that I set my hand to....

A Good Knight in Prison

SIR GUY, *being in the court of a Pagan castle.*

This castle where I dwell, it stands
A long way off from Christian lands,
A long way off my lady's hands,
A long way off the aspen trees,
And murmur of the lime-tree bees.   5

But down the Valley of the Rose
My lady often hawking goes,
Heavy of cheer; oft turns behind,
Leaning towards the western wind,
Because it bringeth to her mind   10
Sad whisperings of happy times,
The face of him who sings these rhymes.

King Guilbert rides beside her there,
Bends low and calls her very fair,
And strives, by pulling down his hair,   15
To hide from my dear lady's ken
The grisly gash I gave him, when
I cut him down at Camelot;
However he strives, he hides it not,
That tourney will not be forgot,   20
Besides, it is King Guilbert's lot,
Whatever he says she answers not.

Now tell me, you that are in love,
From the king's son to the wood-dove,
Which is the better, he or I?   25

For this king means that I should die
In this lone Pagan castle, where
The flowers droop in the bad air
On the September evening.

Look, now I take mine ease and sing,   30
Counting as but a little thing
The foolish spite of a bad king.

For these vile things that hem me in,
These Pagan beasts who live in sin,
The sickly flowers pale and wan,   35
The grim blue-bearded castellan,
The stanchions half worn-out with rust,
Whereto their banner vile they trust—
Why, all these things I hold them just
Like dragons in a missal-book,   40
Wherein, whenever we may look,
We see no horror, yea, delight
We have, the colours are so bright;
Likewise we note the specks of white,
And the great plates of burnish'd gold.   45

Just so this Pagan castle old,
And everything I can see there,
Sick-pining in the marshland air,
I note; I will go over now,
Like one who paints with knitted brow, 50
The flowers and all things one by one,
From the snail on the wall to the setting sun.

Four great walls, and a little one
That leads down to the barbican,
Which walls with many spears they man, 55
When news comes to the castellan
Of Launcelot being in the land.

And as I sit here, close at hand
Four spikes of sad sick sunflowers stand,
The castellan with a long wand 60
Cuts down their leaves as he goes by,
Ponderingly, with screw'd-up eye,
And fingers twisted in his beard—
Nay, was it a knight's shout I heard?
I have a hope makes me afeard: 65
It cannot be, but if some dream
Just for a minute made me deem
I saw among the flowers there
My lady's face with long red hair,
Pale, ivory-colour'd dear face come, 70
As I was wont to see her some
Fading September afternoon,
And kiss me, saying nothing, soon
To leave me by myself again;

Could I get this by longing: vain! 75

The castellan is gone: I see
On one broad yellow flower a bee
Drunk with much honey—

Christ! again,

Some distant knight's voice brings me pain
I thought I had forgot to feel,   80
I never heard the blissful steel
These ten years past: year after year,
Through all my hopeless sojourn here,
No Christian pennon has been near;
Laus Deo! the dragging wind draws on   85
Over the marshes, battle won,
Knights' shouts, and axes hammering,
Yea, quicker now the dint and ring
Of flying hoofs; ah! castellan,
When they come back count man for man,   90
Say whom you miss.

THE PAGANS, *from the battlements.*

Mahound to aid!

Why flee ye so like men dismay'd?

THE PAGANS, *from without.*

Nay, haste! for here is Launcelot,
Who follows quick upon us, hot
And shouting with his men-at-arms.   95

SIR GUY.

Also the Pagans raise alarms,
And ring the bells for fear; at last
My prison walls will be well past.

SIR LAUNCELOT, *from outside.*

Ho! in the name of the Trinity,
Let down the drawbridge quick to me,   100
And open doors, that I may see
Guy the good knight.

93

Nay, Launcelot,
With mere big words ye win us not.

SIR LAUNCELOT.

Bid Miles bring up la perrière,
And archers clear the vile walls there,   105
Bring back the notches to the ear,
Shoot well together! God to aid!
These miscreants will be well paid.

Hurrah! all goes together; Miles
Is good to win my lady's smiles   110
For his good shooting—Launcelot!
On knights a-pace! this game is hot!

SIR GUY *sayeth afterwards.*

I said, I go to meet her now,
And saying so, I felt a blow
From some clench'd hand across my brow,   115
And fell down on the sunflowers
Just as a hammering smote my ears,
After which this I felt in sooth:
My bare hands throttling without ruth
The hairy-throated castellan;   120
Then a grim fight with those that ran
To slay me, while I shouted, 'God
For the Lady Mary!' deep I trod
That evening in my own red blood;
Nevertheless so stiff I stood   125
That when the knights burst the old wood
Of the castle-doors, I was not dead.

I kiss the Lady Mary's head,
Her lips, and her hair golden red,
Because to-day we have been wed.   130

94

The Gilliflower of Gold

A golden gilliflower to-day
I wore upon my helm alway,
And won the prize of this tourney.
 Hah! Hah! la belle jaune giroflée.

However well Sir Giles might sit,   5
His sun was weak to wither it,
Lord Miles's blood was dew on it:
 Hah! Hah! la belle jaune giroflée.

Although my spear in splinters flew
From John's steel-coat, my eye was true;   10
I wheel'd about, and cried for you,
 Hah! Hah! la belle jaune giroflée.

Yea, do not doubt my heart was good,
Though my sword flew like rotten wood,
To shout, although I scarcely stood,   15
 Hah! Hah! la belle jaune giroflée.

My hand was steady too, to take
My axe from round my neck, and break
John's steel-coat up for my love's sake.
 Hah! Hah! la belle jaune giroflée.   20

When I stood in my tent again,
Arming afresh, I felt a pain
Take hold of me, I was so fain—
 Hah! Hah! la belle jaune giroflée.

To hear: '*Honneur aux fils des preux!*'   25
Right in my ears again, and shew
The gilliflower blossom'd new.
 Hah! Hah! la belle jaune giroflée.

95

The Sieur Guillaume against me came,
His tabard bore three points of flame 30
From a red heart: with little blame—
 Hah! Hah! la belle jaune giroflée.

Our tough spears crackled up like straw;
He was the first to turn and draw
His sword, that had nor speck nor flaw,— 35
 Hah! Hah! la belle jaune giroflée.

But I felt weaker than a maid,
And my brain, dizzied and afraid,
Within my helm a fierce tune play'd,—
 Hah! Hah! la belle jaune giroflée. 40

Until I thought of your dear head,
Bow'd to the gilliflower bed,
The yellow flowers stain'd with red;—
 Hah! Hah! la belle jaune giroflée.

Crash! how the swords met, '*giroflée!*' 45
The fierce tune in my helm would play,
'*La belle! la belle! jaune giroflée!*'
 Hah! Hah! la belle jaune giroflée.

Once more the great swords met again,
'*La belle! la belle!*' but who fell then? 50
Le Sieur Guillaume, who struck down ten;—
 Hah! Hah! la belle jaune giroflée.

And as with mazed and unarm'd face,
Toward my own crown and the Queen's place,
They led me at a gentle pace— 55
 Hah! Hah! la belle jaune giroflée.

I almost saw your quiet head
Bow'd o'er the gilliflower bed,
The yellow flowers stain'd with red—
 Hah! Hah! la belle jaune giroflée. 60

Shameful Death

There were four of us about that bed;
    The mass-priest knelt at the side,
I and his mother stood at the head,
    Over his feet lay the bride;
We were quite sure that he was dead,   5
    Though his eyes were open wide.

He did not die in the night,
    He did not die in the day,
But in the morning twilight
    His spirit pass'd away,   10
When neither sun nor moon was bright,
    And the trees were merely grey.

He was not slain with the sword,
    Knight's axe, or the knightly spear,
Yet spoke he never a word   15
    After he came in here;
I cut away the cord
    From the neck of my brother dear.

He did not strike one blow,
    For the recreants came behind,   20
In a place where the hornbeams grow,
    A path right hard to find,
For the hornbeam boughs swing so,
    That the twilight makes it blind.

They lighted a great torch then,   25
    When his arms were pinion'd fast,
Sir John the knight of the Fen,
    Sir Guy of the Dolorous Blast,
With knights threescore and ten,
    Hung brave Lord Hugh at last.   30

I am threescore and ten,
  And my hair is all turn'd grey,
But I met Sir John of the Fen
  Long ago on a summer day,
And am glad to think of the moment when   35
  I took his life away.

I am threescore and ten,
  And my strength is mostly pass'd,
But long ago I and my men,
  When the sky was overcast,   40
And the smoke roll'd over the reeds of the fen,
  Slew Guy of the Dolorous Blast.

And now, knights all of you,
  I pray you pray for Sir Hugh,
A good knight and a true,   45
  And for Alice, his wife, pray too.

The Eve of Crecy

Gold on her head, and gold on her feet,
And gold where the hems of her kirtle meet,
And a golden girdle round my sweet;—
  Ah! qu'elle est belle La Marguerite.

Margaret's maids are fair to see,   5
Freshly dress'd and pleasantly;
Margaret's hair falls down to her knee;—
  Ah! qu'elle est belle La Marguerite.

If I were rich I would kiss her feet,
I would kiss the place where the gold hems meet,   10
And the golden girdle round my sweet—
  Ah! qu'elle est belle La Marguerite.

98

Ah me! I have never touch'd her hand;
When the arrière-ban goes through the land,
Six basnets under my pennon stand;—   15
   Ah! qu'elle est belle La Marguerite.

And many an one grins under his hood:
'Sir Lambert de Bois, with all his men good,
Has neither food nor firewood';—
   Ah! qu'elle est belle La Marguerite.   20

If I were rich I would kiss her feet,
And the golden girdle of my sweet,
And thereabouts where the gold hems meet;—
   Ah! qu'elle est belle La Marguerite.

Yet even now it is good to think,   25
While my few poor varlets grumble and drink
In my desolate hall, where the fires sink,—
   Ah! qu'elle est belle La Marguerite.

Of Margaret sitting glorious there,
In glory of gold and glory of hair,   30
And glory of glorious face most fair;—
   Ah! qu'elle est belle La Marguerite.

Likewise to-night I make good cheer,
Because this battle draweth near:
For what have I to lose or fear?—   35
   Ah! qu'elle est belle La Marguerite.

For, look you, my horse is good to prance
A right fair measure in this war-dance,
Before the eyes of Philip of France;—
   Ah! qu'elle est belle La Marguerite.   40

And sometime it may hap, perdie,
While my new towers stand up three and three,
And my hall gets painted fair to see—
   Ah! qu'elle est belle La Marguerite.

That folks may say: 'Times change, by the rood, 45
For Lambert, banneret of the wood,
Has heaps of food and firewood;—
   Ah! qu'elle est belle La Marguerite.

'And wonderful eyes, too, under the hood
Of a damsel of right noble blood':   50
St Ives, for Lambert of the Wood!—
   Ah! qu'elle est belle La Marguerite.

The Judgment of God

'Swerve to the left, son Roger,' he said,
   'When you catch his eyes through the helmet-slit,
Swerve to the left, then out at his head,
   And the Lord God give you joy of it!'

The blue owls on my father's hood   5
   Were a little dimm'd as I turn'd away;
This giving up of blood for blood
   Will finish here somehow to-day.

So—when I walk'd out from the tent,
   Their howling almost blinded me;   10
Yet for all that I was not bent
   By any shame. Hard by, the sea

Made a noise like the aspens where
   We did that wrong, but now the place
Is very pleasant, and the air   15
   Blows cool on any passer's face.

And all the wrong is gather'd now
   Into the circle of these lists—
Yea, howl out, butchers! tell me how
   His hands were cut off at the wrists;   20

And how Lord Roger bore his face
   A league above his spear-point, high
Above the owls, to that strong place
   Among the waters—yea, yea, cry:

'What a brave champion we have got!   25
   Sir Oliver, the flower of all
The Hainault knights.' The day being hot,
   He sat beneath a broad white pall,

White linen over all his steel;
   What a good knight he look'd! his sword   30
Laid thwart his knees: he liked to feel
   Its steadfast edge clear as his word.

And he look'd solemn; how his love
   Smiled whitely on him, sick with fear!
How all the ladies up above   35
   Twisted their pretty hands! so near

The fighting was—Ellayne! Ellayne!
   They cannot love like you can, who
Would burn your hands off, if that pain
   Could win a kiss—am I not true   40

To you for ever? therefore I
   Do not fear death or anything;
If I should limp home wounded, why,
   While I lay sick you would but sing,

And soothe me into quiet sleep.   45
   If they spat on the recreant knight,
Threw stones at him, and cursed him deep,
   Why then—what then? your hand would light

So gently on his drawn-up face,
   And you would kiss him, and in soft   50
Cool scented clothes would lap him, pace
   The quiet room and weep oft,—oft

Would turn and smile, and brush his cheek
   With your sweet chin and mouth, and in
The order'd garden you would seek   55
   The biggest roses—any sin,

And these say: 'No more now my knight,
   Or God's knight any longer'—you,
Being than they so much more white,
   So much more pure and good and true,   60

Will cling to me for ever—there,
   Is not that wrong turn'd right at last
Through all these years, and I wash'd clean?
   Say, yea, Ellayne; the time is past,

Since on that Christmas-day last year   65
   Up to your feet the fire crept,
And the smoke through the brown leaves sere
   Blinded your dear eyes that you wept;

Was it not I that caught you then,
   And kiss'd you on the saddle bow?   70
Did not the blue owl mark the men
   Whose spears stood like the corn a-row?

This Oliver is a right good knight,
   And must needs beat me, as I fear,
Unless I catch him in the fight,   75
   My father's crafty way—John, here!

Bring up the men from the south gate,
   To help me if I fall or win,
For even if I beat, their hate
   Will grow to more than this mere grin.   80

The Sailing of the Sword

Across the empty garden-beds,
  When the Sword went out to sea,
I scarcely saw my sisters' heads
  Bowed each beside a tree.
I could not see the castle-leads,   5
  When the Sword went out to sea.

Alicia wore a scarlet gown,
  When the Sword went out to sea,
But Ursula's was russet brown:
  For the mist we could not see   10
The scarlet roofs of the good town,
  When the Sword went out to sea.

Green holly in Alicia's hand,
  When the Sword went out to sea;
With sere oak-leaves did Ursula stand;   15
  O! yet alas for me!
I did but bear a peel'd white wand,
  When the Sword went out to sea.

O, russet brown and scarlet bright,
  When the Sword went out to sea,   20
My sisters wore; I wore but white:
  Red, brown and white, are three;
Three damozels; each had a knight,
  When the Sword went out to sea.

Sir Robert shouted loud, and said,   25
  When the Sword went out to sea,
'Alicia, while I see thy head,
  What shall I bring for thee?'
'O, my sweet lord, a ruby red':
  The Sword went out to sea.   30

103

Sir Miles said, while the sails hung down,
When the Sword went out to sea,
'Oh, Ursula! while I see the town,
    What shall I bring for thee?'
'Dear knight, bring back a falcon brown':   35
The Sword went out to sea.

But my Roland, no word he said
When the Sword went out to sea:
But only turn'd away his head,—
    A quick shriek came from me: 40
'Come back, dear lord, to your white maid';—
The Sword went out to sea.

The hot sun bit the garden-beds,
When the Sword came back from sea;
Beneath an apple-tree our heads   45
    Stretched out toward the sea;
Grey gleam'd the thirsty castle-leads,
When the Sword came back from sea.

Lord Robert brought a ruby red,
When the Sword came back from sea;   50
He kissed Alicia on the head:
    'I am come back to thee;
'Tis time, sweet love, that we were wed,
Now the Sword is back from sea!'

Sir Miles he bore a falcon brown,   55
When the Sword came back from sea;
His arms went round tall Ursula's gown,—
    'What joy, O love, but thee?
Let us be wed in the good town,
Now the Sword is back from sea!'   60

My heart grew sick, no more afraid,
  When the Sword came back from sea;
Upon the deck a tall white maid
  Sat on Lord Roland's knee;
His chin was press'd upon her head,   65
  When the Sword came back from sea!

The Haystack in the Floods

Had she come all the way for this,
To part at last without a kiss?
Yea, had she borne the dirt and rain
That her own eyes might see him slain
Beside the haystack in the floods?   5

Along the dripping leafless woods,
The stirrup touching either shoe,
She rode astride as troopers do;
With kirtle kilted to her knee,
To which the mud splash'd wretchedly;   10
And the wet dripp'd from every tree
Upon her head and heavy hair,
And on her eyelids broad and fair;
The tears and rain ran down her face.
By fits and starts they rode apace,   15
And very often was his place
Far off from her; he had to ride
Ahead, to see what might betide
When the roads cross'd; and sometimes, when
There rose a murmuring from his men,   20
Had to turn back with promises;
Ah me! she had but little ease;
And often for pure doubt and dread
She sobb'd, made giddy in the head
By the swift riding; while, for cold,   25
Her slender fingers scarce could hold

The wet reins; yea, and scarcely, too,
She felt the foot within her shoe
Against the stirrup: all for this,
To pass at last without a kiss   30
Beside the haystack in the floods.

For when they near'd that old soak'd hay,
They saw across the only way
That Judas, Godmar, and the three
Red running lions dismally   35
Grinn'd from his pennon, under which,
In one straight line along the ditch,
They counted thirty heads.

               So then,
While Robert turn'd round to his men,
She saw at once the wretched end,   40
And, stooping down, tried hard to rend
Her coif the wrong way from her head,
And hid her eyes; while Robert said:
'Nay, love, 'tis scarcely two to one,
At Poictiers where we made them run   45
So fast—why, sweet my love, good cheer,
The Gascon frontier is so near,
Nought after this.'

             But, 'O,' she said,
'My God! my God! I have to tread
The long way back without you; then   50
The court at Paris; those six men;
The gratings of the Chatelet;
The swift Seine on some rainy day
Like this, and people standing by,
And laughing, while my weak hands try   55
To recollect how strong men swim.
All this, or else a life with him,

For which I should be damned at last,
Would God that this next hour were past!'

He answer'd not, but cried his cry,   60
'St George for Marny!' cheerily;
And laid his hand upon her rein.
Alas! no man of all his train
Gave back that cheery cry again;
And, while for rage his thumb beat fast   65
Upon his sword-hilt, some one cast
About his neck a kerchief long
And bound him.

           Then they went along
To Godmar; who said: 'Now, Jehane,
Your lover's life is on the wane   70
So fast, that, if this very hour
You yield not as my paramour,
He will not see the rain leave off—
Nay, keep your tongue from gibe and scoff,
Sir Robert, or I slay you now.'   75

She laid her hand upon her brow,
Then gazed upon the palm, as though
She thought her forehead bled, and—'No.'
She said, and turned her head away,
As there were nothing else to say,   80
And everything were settled: red
Grew Godmar's face from chin to head:
'Jehane, on yonder hill there stands
My castle, guarding well my lands:
What hinders me from taking you,   85
And doing that I list to do
To your fair wilful body, while
Your knight lies dead?'

A wicked smile
Wrinkled her face, her lips grew thin,
A long way out she thrust her chin: 90
'You know that I should strangle you
While you were sleeping; or bite through
Your throat, by God's help—ah!' she said,
'Lord Jesus, pity your poor maid!
For in such wise they hem me in,   95
I cannot choose but sin and sin,
Whatever happens: yet I think
They could not make me eat or drink,
And so should I just reach my rest.'
'Nay, if you do not my behest,   100
O Jehane! though I love you well,'
Said Godmar, 'would I fail to tell
All that I know?' 'Foul lies,' she said.
'Eh? lies, my Jehane? by God's head,
At Paris folks would deem them true!   105
Do you know, Jehane, they cry for you,
"Jehane the brown! Jehane the brown!
Give us Jehane to burn or drown!"—
Eh—gag me, Robert!—sweet my friend,
This were indeed a piteous end   110
For those long fingers, and long feet,
And long neck, and smooth shoulders sweet;
An end that few men would forget
That saw it—So, an hour yet:
Consider, Jehane, which to take   115
Of life or death!'

              So, scarce awake,
Dismounting, did she leave that place,
And totter some yards: with her face
Turn'd upward to the sky she lay,
Her head on a wet heap of hay,   120

And fell asleep: and while she slept,
And did not dream, the minutes crept
Round to the twelve again; but she,
Being waked at last, sigh'd quietly,
And strangely childlike came, and said: 125
'I will not.' Straightway Godmar's head,
As though it hung on strong wires, turn'd
Most sharply round, and his face burn'd.

For Robert—both his eyes were dry,
He could not weep, but gloomily   130
He seem'd to watch the rain; yea, too,
His lips were firm; he tried once more
To touch her lips; she reached out, sore
And vain desire so tortured them,
The poor grey lips, and now the hem   135
Of his sleeve brush'd them.

                       With a start
Up Godmar rose, thrust them apart;
From Robert's throat he loosed the bands
Of silk and mail; with empty hands
Held out, she stood and gazed, and saw,   140
The long bright blade without a flaw
Glide out from Godmar's sheath, his hand
In Robert's hair; she saw him bend
Back Robert's head; she saw him send
The thin steel down; the blow told well,   145
Right backward the knight Robert fell,
And moan'd as dogs do, being half dead,
Unwitting, as I deem: so then
Godmar turn'd grinning to his men,
Who ran, some five or six, and beat   150
His head to pieces at their feet.

Then Godmar turn'd again and said:
'So, Jehane, the first fitte is read!
Take note, my lady, that your way
Lies backward to the Chatelet!'   155
She shook her head and gazed awhile
At her cold hands with a rueful smile,
As though this thing had made her mad.

This was the parting that they had
Beside the haystack in the floods.   160

Two Red Roses Across the Moon

There was a lady lived in a hall,
Large in the eyes, and slim and tall;
And ever she sung from noon to noon,
Two red roses across the moon.

There was a knight came riding by   5
In early spring, when the roads were dry;
And he heard that lady sing at the noon,
Two red roses across the moon.

Yet none the more he stopp'd at all,
But he rode a-gallop past the hall;   10
And left that lady singing at noon,
Two red roses across the moon.

Because, forsooth, the battle was set,
And the scarlet and blue had got to be met,
He rode on the spur till the next warm noon:— 15
Two red roses across the moon.

But the battle was scatter'd from hill to hill,
From the windmill to the watermill;
And he said to himself, as it near'd the noon,
Two red roses across the moon.   20

You scarce could see for the scarlet and blue,
A golden helm or a golden shoe;
So he cried, as the fight grew thick at the noon,
Two red roses across the moon.

Verily then the gold bore through   25
The huddled spears of the scarlet and blue;
And they cried, as they cut them down at the noon,
Two red roses across the moon.

I trow he stopp'd when he rode again
By the hall, though draggled sore with the rain; 30
And his lips were pinch'd to kiss at the noon
Two red roses across the moon.

Under the may she stoop'd to the crown,
All was gold, there was nothing of brown;
And the horns blew up in the hall at noon,   35
Two red roses across the moon.

Summer Dawn

Pray but one prayer for me 'twixt thy closed lips,
  Think but one thought of me up in the stars.
The summer night waneth, the morning light slips,
  Faint and grey 'twixt the leaves of the aspen, be-
      twixt the cloud-bars,
That are patiently waiting there for the dawn: 5
  Patient and colourless, though Heaven's gold
Waits to float through them along with the sun.

Far out in the meadows, above the young corn,
  The heavy elms wait, and restless and cold
The uneasy wind rises; the roses are dun;   10
Through the long twilight they pray for the dawn,
Round the lone house in the midst of the corn.
  Speak but one word to me over the corn,
  Over the tender, bow'd locks of the corn.

In Prison

Wearily, drearily,
Half the day long,
Flap the great banners
High over the stone;
Strangely and eerily   5
Sounds the wind's song,
Bending the banner-poles.

While, all alone,
Watching the loophole's spark,
Lie I, with life all dark,   10
Feet tether'd, hands fetter'd
Fast to the stone,
The grim walls, square letter'd
With prison'd men's groan.

Still strain the banner-poles   15
Through the wind's song,
Westward the banner rolls
Over my wrong.

From The Life and Death of Jason (Book VI)

And now the Minyae, as they drew anear,
Had been at point to turn about for fear,
Each man beholding his pale fellow's face,
Whose speech was silenced in that dreadful place
By the increasing clamour of the sea   5
And adamantine rocks; then verily
Was Juno good at need, who set strange fire
In Jason's heart, and measureless desire
To be the first of men, and made his voice
Clear as that herald's, whose sweet words rejoice 10

The Gods within the flowery fields of Heaven,
And gave his well-knit arm the strength of seven.
So then, above the crash and thundering,
The Minyae heard his shrill, calm voice, crying:—
'Shall this be, then, an ending to our quest?   15
And shall we find the worst, who sought the best?
Far better had ye sat beside your wives,
And 'mid the wine-cups lingered out your lives,
Dreaming of noble deeds, though trying none,
Than as vain boasters, with your deed undone,   20
Come back to Greece, that men may sing of you.
Are ye all shameless?—are there not a few
Who have slain fear, knowing the unmoved fates
Have meted out already what awaits
The coward and the brave? Ho! Lynceus! stand   25
Upon the prow, and let slip from your hand
The wise king's bird; and all ye note, the wind
Is steady now, and blowing from behind
Drives us toward the clashers, and I hold
The helm myself; therefore, lest we be rolled   30
Broadside against these horrors, take the oar,
And hang here, half a furlong from the shore,
Nor die of fear, until at least we know
If through these gates the Gods will let us go:
And if so be they will not, yet will we   35
Not empty-handed come to Thessaly,
But strike for Æa through this unknown land,
Whose arms reach out to us on either hand.'
    Then they for shame began to cast off fear,
And, handling well the oars, kept Argo near   40
The changing, little-lighted, spray-washed space
Whereunto Lynceus set his eager face,
And loosed the dove, who down the west wind flew;
Then all the others lost her, dashing through

The clouds of spray, but Lynceus noted how   45
She reached the open space, just as a blow
Had spent itself, and still the hollow sound
Of the last clash was booming all around;
And eagerly he noted how the dove
Stopped 'mazed, and hovered for a while above   50
The troubled sea, then stooping, darted through,
As the blue gleaming rocks together drew;
Then scarce he breathed, until a joyous shout
He gave, as he beheld her passing out
Unscathed, above the surface of the sea,   55
While back again the rocks drew sluggishly.
    Then back their poised oars whirled, and straight they
        drave
Unto the opening of the spray-arched cave;
But Jason's eyes alone of all the crew,
Beheld the sunny sea and cloudless blue,   60
Still narrowing, but bright from rock to rock.
    Now as they neared, came the next thundering shock,
That deafened all, and with an icy cloud
Hid man from man; but Jason, shouting loud,
Still clutched the tiller; and the oars, grasped tight   65
By mighty hands, drave on the ship forthright
Unto the rocks, until, with blinded eyes,
They blinked one moment at those mysteries
Unseen before, the next they felt the sun
Full on their backs, and knew their deed was done.   70

Song from Book IV

I know a little garden close
Set thick with lily and red rose,
Where I would wander if I might
From dewy dawn to dewy night,
And have one with me wandering.   5

And though within it no birds sing,
And though no pillared house is there,
And though the apple boughs are bare
Of fruit and blossom, would to God,
Her feet upon the green grass trod, 10
And I beheld them as before.
  There comes a murmur from the shore,
And in the place two fair streams are,
Drawn from the purple hills afar,
Drawn down unto the restless sea; 15
The hills whose flowers ne'er fed the bee,
The shore no ship has ever seen,
Still beaten by the billows green,
Whose murmur comes unceasingly
Unto the place for which I cry. 20
  For which I cry both day and night,
For which I let slip all delight,
That maketh me both deaf and blind,
Careless to win, unskilled to find,
And quick to lose what all men seek. 25
  Yet tottering as I am, and weak,
Still have I left a little breath
To seek within the jaws of death
An entrance to that happy place,
To seek the unforgotten face 30
Once seen, once kissed, once reft from me
Anigh the murmuring of the sea.

From The Earthly Paradise
PRELUDE

Of Heaven or Hell I have no power to sing,
I cannot ease the burden of your fears,
Or make quick-coming death a little thing,
Or bring again the pleasure of past years,

Nor for my words shall ye forget your tears, 5
Or hope again for aught that I can say,
The idle singer of an empty day.

But rather, when aweary of your mirth,
From full hearts still unsatisfied ye sigh,
And, feeling kindly unto all the earth, 10
Grudge every minute as it passes by,
Made the more mindful that the sweet days die—
—Remember me a little then I pray,
The idle singer of an empty day.

The heavy trouble, the bewildering care 15
That weighs us down who live and earn our bread,
These idle verses have no power to bear;
So let me sing of names remembered,
Because they, living not, can ne'er be dead,
Or long time take their memory quite away 20
From us poor singers of an empty day.

Dreamer of dreams, born out of my due time,
Why should I strive to set the crooked straight?
Let it suffice me that my murmuring rhyme
Beats with light wing against the ivory gate, 25
Telling a tale not too importunate
To those who in the sleepy region stay,
Lulled by the singer of an empty day.

Folk say, a wizard to a northern king
At Christmas-tide such wondrous things did shew, 30
That through one window men beheld the spring,
And through another saw the summer glow,
And through a third the fruited vines a-row,
While still, unheard, but in its wonted way,
Piped the drear wind of that December day. 35

So with this Earthly Paradise it is,
If ye will read aright, and pardon me,
Who strive to build a shadowy isle of bliss
Midmost the beating of the steely sea,
Where tossed about all hearts of men must be;   40
Whose ravening monsters mighty men shall slay,
Not the poor singer of an empty day.

The Earthly Paradise. *Atalanta's Race*

I

...And there two runners did the sign abide
Foot set to foot,—a young man slim and fair,
Crisp-haired, well knit, with firm limbs often tried
In places where no man his strength may spare;
Dainty his thin coat was, and on his hair   5
A golden circlet of renown he wore,
And in his hand an olive garland bore.

But on this day with whom shall he contend?
A maid stood by him like Diana clad
When in the woods she lists her bow to bend,   10
Too fair for one to look on and be glad,
Who scarcely yet has thirty summers had,
If he must still behold her from afar;
Too fair to let the world live free from war.

She seemed all earthly matters to forget;   15
Of all tormenting lines her face was clear,
Her wide grey eyes upon the goal were set
Calm and unmoved as though no soul were near,
But her foe trembled as a man in fear,
Nor from her loveliness one moment turned   20
His anxious face with fierce desire that burned.

Now through the hush there broke the trumpet's clang
Just as the setting sun made eventide.
Then from light feet a spurt of dust there sprang,
And swiftly were they running side by side;   25
But silent did the thronging folk abide
Until the turning-post was reached at last,
And round about it still abreast they passed.

But when the people saw how close they ran,
When halfway to the starting-point they were,   30
A cry of joy broke forth, whereat the man
Headed the white-foot runner, and drew near
Unto the very end of all his fear;
And scarce his straining feet the ground could feel,
And bliss unhoped for o'er his heart 'gan steal.   35

But midst the loud victorious shouts he heard
Her footsteps drawing nearer, and the sound
Of fluttering raiment, and thereat afeard
His flushed and eager face he turned around,
And even then he felt her past him bound   40
Fleet as the wind, but scarcely saw her there
Till on the goal she laid her fingers fair.

There stood she breathing like a little child
Amid some warlike clamour laid asleep,
For no victorious joy her red lips smiled,   45
Her cheek its wonted freshness did but keep;
No glance lit up her clear grey eyes and deep,
Though some divine thought softened all her face
As once more rang the trumpet through the place.

But her late foe stopped short amidst his course,   50
One moment gazed upon her piteously,
Then with a groan his lingering feet did force

To leave the spot whence he her eyes could see;
And, changed like one who knows his time must be
But short and bitter, without any word   55
He knelt before the bearer of the sword;

  Then high rose up the gleaming deadly blade,
Bared of its flowers, and through the crowded place
Was silence now, and midst of it the maid
Went by the poor wretch at a gentle pace,   60
And he to hers upturned his sad white face;
Nor did his eyes behold another sight
Ere on his soul there fell eternal night.

II

...Now has the lingering month at last gone by,
Again are all folk round the running place,   65
Nor other seems the dismal pageantry
Than heretofore, but that another face
Looks o'er the smooth course ready for the race,
For now, beheld of all, Milanion
Stands on the spot he twice has looked upon.   70

  But yet—what change is this that holds the maid?
Does she indeed see in his glittering eye
More than disdain of the sharp shearing blade,
Some happy hope of help and victory?
The others seemed to say, 'We come to die,   75
Look down upon us for a little while,
That dead, we may bethink us of thy smile.'

  But he—what look of mastery was this
He cast on her? why were his lips so red?
Why was his face so flushed with happiness?   80
So looks not one who deems himself but dead,
E'en if to death he bows a willing head;
So rather looks a god well pleased to find
Some earthly damsel fashioned to his mind.

Why must she drop her lids before his gaze,   85
And even as she casts adown her eyes
Redden to note his eager glance of praise,
And wish that she were clad in other guise?
Why must the memory to her heart arise
Of things unnoticed when they first were heard,   90
Some lover's song, some answering maiden's word?

What makes these longings, vague, without a name,
And this vain pity never felt before,
This sudden languor, this contempt of fame,
This tender sorrow for the time past o'er,   95
These doubts that grow each minute more and more?
Why does she tremble as the time grows near,
And weak defeat and woeful victory fear?

Now while she seemed to hear her beating heart,
Above their heads the trumpet blast rang out   100
And forth they sprang; and she must play her part.
Then flew her white feet, knowing not a doubt,
Though slackening once, she turned her head about,
But then she cried aloud and faster fled
Than e'er before, and all men deemed him dead.   105

But with no sound he raised aloft his hand,
And thence what seemed a ray of light there flew
And past the maid rolled on along the sand;
Then trembling she her feet together drew
And in her heart a strong desire there grew   110
To have the toy: some god she thought had given
That gift to her, to make of earth a heaven.

Then from the course with eager steps she ran,
And in her odorous bosom laid the gold.
But when she turned again, the great-limbed man,   115

Now well ahead she failed not to behold,
And mindful of her glory waxing cold,
Sprang up and followed him in hot pursuit,
Though with one hand she touched the golden fruit.

Note too, the bow that she was wont to bear　120
She laid aside to grasp the glittering prize,
And o'er her shoulder from the quiver fair
Three arrows fell and lay before her eyes
Unnoticed, as amidst the people's cries
She sprang to head the strong Milanion,　　125
Who now the turning-post had well-nigh won.

But as he set his mighty hand on it
White fingers underneath his own were laid,
And white limbs from his dazzled eyes did flit,
Then he the second fruit cast by the maid,　　130
She ran awhile, and then as one afraid
Wavered and stopped, and turned, and made no stay,
Until the globe with its bright fellow lay.

Then as a troubled glance she cast around
Now far ahead the Argive could she see,　　135
And in her garment's hem one hand she wound
To keep the double prize, and strenuously
Sped o'er the course, and little doubt had she
To win the day, though now but scanty space
Was left betwixt him and the winning place.　　140

Short was the way unto such winged feet,
Quickly she gained upon him till at last
He turned about her eager eyes to meet
And from his hand the third fair apple cast.
She wavered not, but turned and ran so fast　　145
After the prize that should her bliss fulfil,
That in her hand it lay ere it was still.

Nor did she rest, but turned about to win
Once more, an unblest woeful victory—
And yet—and yet—why does her breath begin   150
To fail her, and her feet drag heavily?
Why fails she now to see if far or nigh
The goal is? why do her grey eyes grow dim?
Why do these tremors run through every limb?

She spreads her arms abroad some stay to find   155
Else must she fall, indeed, and findeth this,
A strong man's arms about her body twined,
Nor may she shudder now to feel his kiss,
So wrapped she is in new unbroken bliss:
Made happy that the foe the prize hath won,   160
She weeps glad tears for all her glory done.

Shatter the trumpet, hew adown the posts!
Upon the brazen altar break the sword,
And scatter incense to appease the ghosts
Of those who died here by their own award.   165
Bring forth the image of the mighty Lord,
And her who unseen o'er the runners hung,
And did a deed for ever to be sung.

Here are the gathered folk, make no delay,
Open King Schœneus' well-filled treasury,   170
Bring out the gifts long hid from light of day,
The golden bowls o'erwrought with imagery,
Gold chains, and unguents brought from over sea,
The saffron gown the old Phœnician brought,
Within the temple of the Goddess wrought.   175

O ye, O damsels, who shall never see
Her, that Love's servant bringeth now to you,
Returning from another victory,

In some cool bower do all that now is due!
Since she in token of her service new   180
Shall give to Venus offerings rich enow,
Her maiden zone, her arrows, and her bow.

From The Man Born to be King

Long time he rode, till suddenly,
When now the sun was broad and high,
From out the hollow where the yew
Still guarded patches of the dew,
He rode and saw that he had won   5
That highland's edge, and gazed upon
A valley that beneath the haze
Of that most fair of autumn days,
Showed glorious; fair with golden sheaves,
Rich with darkened autumn-leaves,   10
Gay with the water-meadows green,
The bright blue streams that lay between,
The miles of beauty stretched away
From that bleak hill-side bare and grey.
Till white cliffs over slopes of vine,   15
Drew 'gainst the sky a broken line.
And 'twixt the vineyards and the stream
Michael saw gilded spirelets gleam;
For, hedged with many a flowery close,
There lay the Castle of the Rose,   20
His hurried journey's aim and end.

Then downward he began to wend,
And 'twixt the flowery hedges sweet
He heard the hook smite down the wheat,
And murmur of the unseen folk;   25
But when he reached the stream that broke

The golden plain, but leisurely
He passed the bridge, for he could see
The masters of that ripening realm,
Cast down beneath an ancient elm   30
Upon a little strip of grass,
From hand to hand the pitcher pass,
While on the ground beside them lay
The ashen-handled sickles grey,
The matters of their cheer between: 35
Slices of white cheese, specked with green,
And greenstriped onions and ryebread,
And summer apples faintly red,
Even beneath the crimson skin;
And yellow grapes, well ripe and thin,   40
Plucked from the cottage gable-end.

And certes Michael felt their friend
Hearing their voices, nor forgot
His boyhood and the pleasant spot
Beside the well-remembered stream;   45
And friendly did this water seem
As through its white-flowered weeds it ran
Bearing good things to beast and man.
    Yea, as the parapet he passed,
And they a greeting toward him cast,   50
Once more he felt a boy again;
As though beneath the harvest wain
He was asleep, by that old stream,
And all these things were but a dream—
The King, the Squire, the hurrying ride   55
Unto the lonely quagmire side;
The sudden pain, the deadly swoon,
The feverish life from noon to noon;
The tending of the kind old man,
The black and white Dominican,   60

The hour before the Abbot's throne,
The poring o'er old books alone,
In summer morns; the King again,
The envious greetings of strange men,
This mighty horse and rich array, 65
This journey on an unknown way.
  Surely he thought to wake from it,
And once more by the waggon sit,
Blinking upon the sunny mill.
  But not for either good or ill 70
Shall he see one of all those days;
On through the quivering noontide haze
He rode, and now on either hand
Heavy with fruit the trees did stand;
Nor had he ridden long, ere he 75
The red towers of the house could see
Grey on the wind-beat southern side:
And soon the gates thrown open wide
He saw, the long-fixed drawbridge down,
The moat, with lilies overgrown, 80
Midst which the gold-scaled fishes lay:
Such peace was there for many a day.

From The Earthly Paradise

L'ENVOI

Here are we for the last time face to face,
Thou and I, Book, before I bid thee speed
Upon thy perilous journey to that place
For which I have done on thee pilgrim's weed,
Striving to get thee all things for thy need— 5
—I love thee, whatso time or men may say
Of the poor singer of an empty day.

Good reason why I love thee, e'en if thou
Be mocked or clean forgot as time wears on;
For ever as thy fashioning did grow,   10
Kind word and praise because of thee I won
From those without whom were my world all gone,
My hope fallen dead, my singing cast away,
And I set soothly in an empty day.

I love thee; yet this last time must it be   15
That thou must hold thy peace and I must speak,
Lest if thou babble I begin to see
Thy gear too thin, thy limbs and heart too weak,
To find the land thou goest forth to seek—
—Though what harm if thou die upon the way,   20
Thou idle singer of an empty day?

But though this land desired thou never reach,
Yet folk who know it mayst thou meet or death;
Therefore a word unto thee would I teach
To answer these, who, noting thy weak breath,   25
Thy wandering eyes, thy heart of little faith,
May make thy fond desire a sport and play,
Mocking the singer of an empty day.

That land's name, say'st thou? and the road thereto?
Nay, Book, thou mockest, saying thou know'st it not;   30
Surely no book of verse I ever knew
But ever was the heart within him hot
To gain the Land of Matters Unforgot—
—There, now we both laugh—as the whole world may,
At us poor singers of an empty day.   35

Nay, let it pass, and hearken! Hast thou heard
That therein I believe I have a friend,
Of whom for love I may not be afeard?
It is to him indeed I bid thee wend;

Yea, he perchance may meet thee ere thou end,　　40
Dying so far off from the hedge of bay,
Thou idle singer of an empty day!

Well, think of him, I bid thee, on the road,
And if it hap that midst of thy defeat,
Fainting beneath thy follies' heavy load,　　　　45
My Master, GEOFFREY CHAUCER, thou do meet,
Then shalt thou win a space of rest full sweet;
Then be thou bold, and speak the words I say.
The idle singer of an empty day!

'O Master, O thou great of heart and tongue,　50
Thou well mayst ask me why I wander here,
In raiment rent of stories oft besung!
But of thy gentleness draw thou anear,
And then the heart of one who held thee dear
Mayst thou behold! So near as that I lay　　　55
Unto the singer of an empty day.

'For this he ever said, who sent me forth
To seek a place amid thy company;
That howsoever little was my worth,
Yet was he worth e'en just so much as I;　　　60
He said that rhyme hath little skill to lie;
Nor feigned to cast his worser part away
In idle singing for an empty day.

'I have beheld him tremble oft enough
At things he could not choose but trust to me,　65
Although he knew the world was wise and rough:
And never did he fail to let me see
His love,—his folly and faithlessness, maybe;
And still in turn I gave him voice to pray
Such prayers as cling about an empty day...　　70

*　　*　　*　　*　　*

'O Master, if thine heart could love us yet,
Spite of things left undone, and wrongly done,
Some place in loving hearts then should we get,
For thou, sweet-souled, didst never stand alone,
But knew'st the joy and woe of many an one—   75
—By lovers dead, who live through thee, we pray,
Help thou us singers of an empty day!'

Fearest thou, Book, what answer thou mayst gain
Lest he should scorn thee, and thereof thou die?
Nay, it shall not be.—Thou mayst toil in vain,   80
And never draw the House of Fame anigh;
Yet he and his shall know whereof we cry,
Shall call it not ill done to strive to lay
The ghosts that crowd about life's empty day.

Then let the others go! and if indeed   85
In some old garden thou and I have wrought,
And made fresh flowers spring up from hoarded seed,
And fragrance of old days and deeds have brought
Back to folk weary; all was not for nought.
—No little part it was for me to play—   90
The idle singer of an empty day.

From Love is Enough

THE MUSIC

LOVE IS ENOUGH: ho ye who seek saving,
   Go no further; come hither; there have been who have
      found it,
And these know the House of Fulfilment of Craving;
   These know the Cup with the roses around it;
   These know the World's Wound and the balm that
      hath bound it: 5
Cry out, the World heedeth not, 'Love lead us home!'

He leadeth, He hearkeneth, He cometh to you-ward;
Set your faces as steel to the fears that assemble
Round his goad for the faint, and his scourge for the
    froward:
Lo his lips, how with tales of last kisses they tremble! 10
Lo his eyes of all sorrow that may not dissemble!
Cry out, for he heedeth, 'O Love, lead us home!'

O hearken the words of his voice of compassion:
    'Come cling round about me, ye faithful who sicken
Of the weary unrest and the world's passing fashion! 15
    As the rain in mid-morning your troubles shall thicken,
    But surely within you some Godhead doth quicken,
As ye cry to me heeding, and leading you home.

'Come—pain ye shall have, and be blind to the ending!
    Come—fear ye shall have, mid the sky's overcasting! 20
Come—change ye shall have, for far are ye wending!
    Come—no crown ye shall have for your thirst and your
        fasting,
    But the kissed lips of Love and fair life everlasting!
Cry out, for one heedeth, who leadeth you home!'

Is he gone? was he with us?—ho ye who seek saving, 25
    Go no further; come hither; for have we not found it?
Here is the House of Fulfilment of Craving;
    Here is the Cup with the roses around it;
    The World's Wound well healed, and the balm that
        hath bound it:
Cry out! for he heedeth, fair Love that led home. 30

From Sigurd the Volsung

Sigmund receiveth his Sword from Odin.

So round about the Branstock they feast in the gleam of
the gold;
And though the deeds of man-folk were not yet waxen
old,
Yet had they tales for songcraft, and the blossomed garth
of rhyme;
Tales of the framing of all things and the entering in of
time
From the halls of the outer heaven; so near they knew
the door.   5
Wherefore uprose a sea-king, and his hands that loved the
oar
Now dealt with the rippling harp-gold, and he sang of the
shaping of earth,
And how the stars were lighted, and where the winds had
birth,
And the gleam of the first of summers on the yet untrodden
grass.
But e'en as men's hearts were hearkening some heard the
thunder pass   10
O'er the cloudless noontide heaven; and some men turned
about
And deemed that in the doorway they heard a man laugh
out.
Then into the Volsung dwelling a mighty man there strode,
One-eyed and seeming ancient, yet bright his visage
glowed:
Cloud-blue was the hood upon him, and his kirtle gleaming-
grey   15
As the latter morning sundog when the storm is on the
way:

A bill he bore on his shoulder, whose mighty ashen beam
Burnt bright with the flame of the sea and the blended
   silver's gleam.
And such was the guise of his raiment as the Volsung
   elders had told
Was borne by their fathers' fathers, and the first that
   warred in the wold.   20

So strode he to the Branstock nor greeted any lord,
But forth from his cloudy raiment he drew a gleaming
   sword,
And smote it deep in the tree-bole, and the wild hawks
   overhead
Laughed 'neath the naked heaven as at last he spake and
   said:
'Earls of the Goths, and Volsungs, abiders on the earth, 25
Lo there amid the Branstock a blade of plenteous worth!
The folk of the war-wand's forgers wrought never better
   steel
Since first the burg of heaven uprose for man-folk's weal.
Now let the man among you whose heart and hand may
   shift
To pluck it from the oakwood e'en take it for my gift. 30
Then ne'er, but his own heart falter, its point and edge
   shall fail
Until the night's beginning and the ending of the tale.
Be merry, Earls of the Goth-folk, O Volsung Sons, be
   wise,
And reap the battle-acre that ripening for you lies:
For they told me in the wild wood, I heard on the moun-
   tain side   35
That the shining house of heaven is wrought exceeding
   wide,
And that there the Early-comers shall have abundant rest

While Earth grows scant of great ones, and fadeth from
　　its best,
And fadeth from its midward and groweth poor and vile :—
All hail to thee, King Volsung! farewell for a little
　　while!'　　　　　　　　　　　　　　　　　　　40

So sweet his speaking sounded, so wise his words did seem
That moveless all men sat there, as in a happy dream
We stir not lest we waken; but there his speech had end,
And slowly down the hall-floor, and outward did he wend;
And none would cast him a question or follow on his
　　ways,　　　　　　　　　　　　　　　　　　　45
For they knew that the gift was Odin's, a sword for the
　　world to praise.

But now spake Volsung the King: 'Why sit ye silent
　　and still?
Is the Battle-Father's visage a token of terror and ill?
Arise, O Volsung Children, Earls of the Goths, arise,
And set your hands to the hilts as mighty men and
　　wise!　　　　　　　　　　　　　　　　　　　50
Yet deem it not too easy; for belike a fateful blade
Lies there in the heart of the Branstock for a fated warrior
　　made.'

Now therewith spake King Siggeir: 'King Volsung, give
　　me a grace
To try it the first of all men, lest another win my place
And mere chance-hap steal my glory and the gain that I
　　might win.'　　　　　　　　　　　　　　　　55
Then somewhat laughed King Volsung, and he said:
　　'O Guest, begin ;
Though herein is the first as the last, for the Gods have
　　long to live,
Nor hath Odin yet forgotten unto whom the gift he would
　　give.'

Then forth to the tree went Siggeir, the Goth-folk's
mighty lord,
And laid his hand on the gemstones, and strained at the
glorious sword   60
Till his heart grew black with anger; and never a word
he said
As he wended back to the high-seat: but Signy waxed
blood-red
When he sat him adown beside her: and her heart was
nigh to break
For the shame and the fateful boding: and therewith
King Volsung spake:

'Thus comes back empty-handed the mightiest King of
Earth,   65
And how shall the feeble venture? yet each man knows
his worth;
And to-day may a great beginning from a little seed upspring
To o'erpass many a great one that hath the name of King:
So stand forth free and unfree; stand forth both most and
least:
But first ye Earls of the Goth-folk, ye lovely lords we
feast.'   70

Upstood the Earls of Siggeir, and each man drew anigh
And deemed his time was coming for a glorious gain and
high;
But for all their mighty shaping and their deeds in the
battle-wood,
No looser in the Branstock that gift of Odin stood.
Then uprose Volsung's homemen, and the fell-abiding
folk;   75
And the yellow-headed shepherds came gathering round
the Oak,
And the searchers of the thicket and the dealers with the oar:

And the least and the worst of them all was a mighty man
of war.
But for all their mighty shaping, and the struggle and the
strain
Of their hands, the deft in labour, they tugged thereat in
vain;   80
And still as the shouting and jeers, and the names of men
and the laughter
Beat backward from gable to gable, and rattled o'er roof-
tree and rafter,
Moody and still sat Siggeir; for he said: 'They have
trained me here
As a mock for their woodland bondsmen; and yet they
shall buy it dear.'

Now the tumult sank a little, and men cried on Volsung
the King   85
And his sons, the hedge of battle, to try the fateful thing.
So Volsung laughed, and answered: 'I will set me to the
toil,
Lest these my guests of the Goth-folk should deem I fear
the foil.
Yet nought am I ill-sworded, and the oldest friend is best;
And this, my hand's first fellow, will I bear to the grave-
mound's rest,   90
Nor wield meanwhile another: Yea, this shall I have in
hand
When mid the host of Odin in the Day of Doom I stand.'

Therewith from his belt of battle he raised the golden
sheath,
And showed the peace-strings glittering about the hidden
death:
Then he laid his hand on the Branstock, and cried: 'O
tree beloved,   95

134

I thank thee of thy good-heart that so little thou art moved:
Abide thou thus, green bower, when I am dead and gone
And the best of all my kindred a better day hath won!'

Then as a young man laughed he, and on the hilts of gold
His hand, the battle-breaker, took fast and certain hold, 100
And long he drew and strained him, but mended not the
    tale,
Yet none the more thereover his mirth of heart did fail;
But he wended to the high-seat and thence began to cry:

'Sons I have gotten and cherished, now stand ye forth to
    try;
Lest Odin tell in God-home how from the way he
    strayed, 105
And how to the man he would not he gave away his
    blade.'
So therewithal rose Rerir, and wasted might and main;
Then Gunthiof, and then Hunthiof, they wearied them in
    vain;
Nought was the might of Agnar; nought Helgi could
    avail;
Sigi the tall and Solar no further brought the tale, 110
Nor Geirmund the priest of the temple, nor Gylfi of
    the wood.

At last by the side of the Branstock Sigmund the Volsung
    stood,
And with right hand wise in battle the precious sword-hilt
    caught,
Yet in a careless fashion, as he deemed it all for nought:
When lo, from floor to rafter went up a shattering
    shout, 115
For aloft in the hand of Sigmund the naked blade shone
    out

As high o'er his head he shook it: for the sword had come away

From the grip of the heart of the Branstock, as though all loose it lay.

A little while he stood there mid the glory of the hall,

Like the best of the trees of the garden, when the April sunbeams fall   120

On its blossomed boughs in the morning, and tell of the days to be;

Then back unto the high-seat he wended soberly:

For this was the thought within him: Belike the day shall come

When I shall bide here lonely amid the Volsung home,

Its glory and sole avenger, its after-summer seed.   125

Yea, I am the hired of Odin, his workday will to speed,

And the harvest-tide shall be heavy.—What then, were it come and past,

And I laid by the last of the sheaves with my wages earned at the last?

He lifted his eyes as he thought it, for now was he come to his place

And there he stood by his father and met Siggeir face to face...   130

Sigurd getteth to him the horse that is called Greyfell.

...Then again gat Sigurd outward, and adown the steep he ran

And unto the horse-fed meadow: but lo, a grey-clad man,

One-eyed and seeming ancient, there met him by the way:

And he spake: 'Thou hastest, Sigurd; yet tarry till I say

A word that shall well bestead thee: for I know of these
    mountains well   135
And all the lea of Gripir, and the beasts that thereon
    dwell.'

'Wouldst thou have red gold for thy tidings? art thou
    Gripir's horse-herd then?
Nay sure, for thy face is shining like the battle-eager men
My master Regin tells of: and I love thy cloud-grey gown,
And thy visage gleams above it like a thing my dreams
    have known.'   140

'Nay, whiles have I heeded the horse-kind,' then spake
    that elder of days,
'And sooth do the sages say, when the beasts of my
    breeding they praise.
There is one thereof in the meadow, and, wouldst thou
    cull him out,
Thou shalt follow an elder's counsel, who hath brought
    strange things about,
Who hath known thy father aforetime, and other kings
    of thy kin.'   145

So Sigurd said, 'I am ready; and what is the deed to
    win?'
He said: 'We shall drive the horses adown to the water-
    side,
That cometh forth from the mountains, and note what
    next shall betide.'

Then the twain sped on together, and they drave the
    horses on
Till they came to a rushing river, a water wide and
    wan;   150

137

And the white mews hovered o'er it; but none might hear
  their cry
For the rush and rattle of waters, as the downlong flood
  swept by.
So the whole herd took the river and strove the stream to
  stem,
And many a brave steed was there; but the flood
  o'ermastered them:
And some, it swept them down-ward, and some won back
  to bank,   155
Some, caught by the net of the eddies, in the swirling
  hubbub sank;
But one of all swam over, and they saw his mane of grey
Toss over the flowery meadows, a bright thing far away:
Wide then he wheeled about them, then took the stream
  again
And with the waves' white horses mingled his cloudy
  mane.   160

Then spake the elder of days: 'Hearken now, Sigurd, and
  hear;
Time was when I gave thy father a gift thou shalt yet
  deem dear,
And this horse is a gift of my giving:—heed nought
  where thou mayst ride:
For I have seen thy fathers in a shining house abide,
And on earth they thought of its threshold, and the gifts
  I had to give;   165
Nor prayed for a little longer, and a little longer to live.'

Then forth he strode to the mountains, and fain was
  Sigurd now
To ask him many a matter: but dim did his bright shape
  grow,

As a man from the litten doorway fades into the dusk of
 night;
And the sun in the high-noon shone, and the world was
 exceeding bright.   170
So Sigurd turned to the river and stood by the wave-wet
 strand,
And the grey horse swims to his feet and lightly leaps
 aland,
And the youngling looks upon him, and deems none
 beside him good.
And indeed, as tells the story, he was come of Sleipnir's
 blood,
The tireless horse of Odin: cloud-grey he was of hue, 175
And it seemed as Sigurd backed him that Sigmund's son
 he knew,
So glad he went beneath him. Then the youngling's song
 arose
As he brushed through the noontide blossoms of Gripir's
 mighty close,
Then he singeth the song of Greyfell, the horse that Odin
 gave,
Who swam through the sweeping river, and back through
 the toppling wave.   180

How Sigurd awoke Brynhild upon Hindfell.
*   *   *   *   *

Night falls, but yet rides Sigurd, and hath no thought of
 rest,
For he longs to climb that rock-world and behold the earth
 at its best;
But now mid the maze of the foot-hills he seeth the light
 no more,
And the stars are lovely and gleaming on the lightless
 heavenly floor.

139

So up and up he wendeth till the night is wearing thin; 185
And he rideth a rift of the mountain, and all is dark therein,
Till the stars are dimmed by dawning and the wakening
  world is cold;
Then afar in the upper rock-wall a breach doth he behold,
And a flood of light poured inward the doubtful dawning
  blinds:
So swift he rideth thither and the mouth of the breach he
  finds,   190
And sitteth awhile on Greyfell on the marvellous thing to
  gaze:
For lo, the side of Hindfell enwrapped by the fervent
  blaze,
And nought 'twixt earth and heaven save a world of
  flickering flame,
And a hurrying shifting tangle, where the dark rents went
  and came.

Great groweth the heart of Sigurd with uttermost de-
  sire,   195
And he crieth kind to Greyfell, and they hasten up, and
  nigher,
Till he draweth rein in the dawning on the face of
  Hindfell's steep:
But who shall heed the dawning where the tongues of that
  wildfire leap?
For they weave a wavering wall, that driveth over the
  heaven
The wind that is born within it; nor ever aside is it
  driven   200
By the mightiest wind of the waste, and the rain-flood
  amidst it is nought;
And no wayfarer's door and no window the hand of its
  builder hath wrought.

But thereon is the Volsung smiling as its breath uplifteth
his hair,

And his eyes shine bright with its image, and his mail
gleams white and fair,

And his war-helm pictures the heavens and the waning
stars behind: 205

But his neck is Greyfell stretching to snuff at the flame-
wall blind,

And his cloudy flank upheaveth, and tinkleth the knitted
mail,

And the gold of the uttermost waters is waxen wan and
pale.

Now Sigurd turns in his saddle, and the hilt of the Wrath
he shifts,

And draws a girth the tighter; then the gathered reins he
lifts,   210

And crieth aloud to Greyfell, and rides at the wildfire's
heart;

But the white wall wavers before him and the flame-flood
rusheth apart,

And high o'er his head it riseth, and wide and wild is its
roar

As it beareth the mighty tidings to the very heavenly
floor:

But he rideth through its roaring as the warrior rides the
rye,   215

When it bows with the wind of the summer and the hid
spears draw anigh;

The white flame licks his raiment and sweeps through
Greyfell's mane,

And bathes both hands of Sigurd and the hilts of Fafnir's
bane,

And winds about his war-helm and mingles with his hair,
But nought his raiment dusketh or dims his glittering
    gear;   220
Then it fails and fades and darkens till all seems left
    behind,
And dawn and the blaze is swallowed in mid-mirk stark
    and blind.

But forth a little further and a little further on
And all is calm about him, and he sees the scorched earth
    wan
Beneath a glimmering twilight, and he turns his conquering
    eyes,   225
And a ring of pale slaked ashes on the side of Hindfell
    lies;
And the world of the waste is beyond it; and all is hushed
    and grey,
And the new-risen moon is a-paleing, and the stars grow
    faint with day.

Then Sigurd looked before him and a Shield-burg there he
    saw,
A wall of the tiles of Odin wrought clear without a
    flaw,   230
The gold by the silver gleaming, and the ruddy by the
    white;
And the blazonings of their glory were done upon them
    bright,
As of dear things wrought for the war-lords new come to
    Odin's hall;
Piled high aloft to the heavens uprose that battle-wall,
And far o'er the topmost shield-rim for a banner of fame
    there hung   235
A glorious golden buckler; and against the staff it rung

As the earliest wind of dawning uprose on Hindfell's
    face
And the light from the yellowing east beamed soft on the
    shielded place.

*   *   *   *   *

So there was Sigurd alone; and he went from the shielded
    door,
And aloft in the desert of wonder the Light of the
    Branstock he bore;   240
And he set his face to the earth-mound, and beheld the
    image wan,
And the dawn was growing about it; and, lo, the shape of
    a man
Set forth to the eyeless desert on the tower-top of the
    world,
High over the cloud-wrought castle whence the windy
    bolts are hurled.

*   *   *   *   *

Now over the body he standeth, and seeth it shapen
    fair,   245
And clad from head to foot-sole in pale grey-glittering gear,
In a hauberk wrought as straitly as though to the flesh it
    were grown:
But a great helm hideth the head and is girt with a
    glittering crown.
So thereby he stoopeth and kneeleth, for he deems it were
    good indeed
If the breath of life abide there and the speech to help at
    need;   250
And as sweet as the summer wind from a garden under the
    sun
Cometh forth on the topmost Hindfell the breath of that
    sleeping-one.

Then he saith he will look on the face, if it bear him love
or hate,
Or the bonds for his life's constraining, or the sundering
doom of fate.

So he draweth the helm from the head, and, lo, the brow
snow-white, 255
And the smooth unfurrowed cheeks, and the wise lips
breathing light;
And the face of a woman it is, and the fairest that ever was
born,
Shown forth to the empty heavens and the desert world
forlorn:
But he looketh, and loveth her sore, and he longeth her
spirit to move,
And awaken her heart to the world, that she may behold
him and love. 260
And he toucheth her breast and her hands, and he loveth
her passing sore;
And he saith: 'Awake! I am Sigurd'; but she moveth
never the more.
Then he looked on his bare bright blade, and he said:
'Thou—what wilt thou do?
For indeed as I came by the war-garth thy voice of desire
I knew.'
Bright burnt the pale blue edges, for the sunrise drew
anear, 265
And the rims of the Shield-burg glittered, and the east was
exceeding clear:

So the eager edges he setteth to the Dwarf-wrought battle-
coat
Where the hammered ring-knit collar constraineth the
woman's throat;

But the sharp Wrath biteth and rendeth, and before it fail
the rings,
And, lo, the gleam of the linen, and the light of golden
things; 270
Then he driveth the blue steel onward, and through the
skirt, and out,
Till nought but the rippling linen is wrapping her about;
Then he deems her breath comes quicker and her breast
begins to heave,
So he turns about the War-Flame and rends down either
sleeve,
Till her arms lie white in her raiment, and a river of sun-
bright hair 275
Flows free o'er bosom and shoulder and floods the desert
bare.

Then a flush cometh over her visage and a sigh up-heaveth
her breast,
And her eyelids quiver and open, and she wakeneth into
rest;
Wide-eyed on the dawning she gazeth, too glad to change
or smile,
And but little moveth her body, nor speaketh she yet for
a while; 280
And yet kneels Sigurd moveless her wakening speech to
heed,
While soft the waves of the daylight o'er the starless
heavens speed,
And the gleaming rims of the Shield-burg yet bright and
brighter grow,
And the thin moon hangeth her horns dead-white in the
golden-glow.

Then she turned and gazed on Sigurd, and her eyes met
the Volsung's eyes. 285

And mighty and measureless now did the tide of his love
arise,
For their longing had met and mingled, and he knew of
her heart that she loved,
As she spake unto nothing but him and her lips with the
speech-flood moved:
'O, what is the thing so mighty that my weary sleep hath
torn,
And rent the fallow bondage, and the wan woe over-
worn?'   290

He said: 'The hand of Sigurd and the sword of Sigmund's
son,
And the heart that the Volsungs fashioned this deed for
thee have done.'

But she said: 'Where then is Odin that laid me here alow?
Long lasteth the grief of the world, and manfolk's tangled
woe!'

'He dwelleth above,' said Sigurd, 'but I on the earth
abide,   295
And I came from the Glittering Heath the waves of thy
fire to ride.'

*   *   *   *   *

Then Sigurd looketh upon her, and the words from his
heart arise:
'Thou art the fairest of earth, and the wisest of the wise;
O who art thou that lovest? I am Sigurd, e'en as I told;
I have slain the Foe of the Gods, and gotten the Ancient
Gold;   300
And great were the gain of thy love, and the gift of mine
earthly days,
If we twain should never sunder as we wend on the
changing ways.

146

O who art thou that lovest, thou fairest of all things born?
And what meaneth thy sleep and thy slumber in the
wilderness forlorn?'

The Last of Sigurd.

*   *   *   *   *

There is peace on the bale of Sigurd, and the Gods look
    down from on high,   305
And they see the lids of the Volsung close shut against the
    sky,
As he lies with his shield beside him in the Hauberk all of
    gold,
That has not its like in the heavens, nor has earth of its
    fellow told;
And forth from the Helm of Aweing are the sunbeams
    flashing wide,
And the sheathèd Wrath of Sigurd lies still by his mighty
    side.   310
Then cometh an elder of days, a man of the ancient times,
Who is long past sorrow and joy, and the steep of the bale
    he climbs;
And he kneeleth down by Sigurd, and bareth the Wrath
    to the sun
That the beams are gathered about it, and from hilt to
    blood-point run,
And wide o'er the plains of the Niblungs doth the Light
    of the Branstock glare,   315
Till the wondering mountain-shepherds on that star of
    noontide stare,
And fear for many an evil; but the ancient man stands
    still
With the war-flame on his shoulder, nor thinks of good or
    of ill,

Till the feet of Brynhild's bearers on the topmost bale are
laid,
And her bed is dight by Sigurd's; then he sinks the pale
white blade   320
And lays it 'twixt the sleepers, and leaves them there
alone—
He, the last that shall ever behold them,—and his days are
well nigh done.

Then is silence over the plain; in the noon shine the
torches pale
As the best of the Niblung Earl-folk bear fire to the builded
bale:
Then a wind in the west ariseth, and the white flames leap
on high,   325
And with one voice crieth the people a great and mighty
cry,
And men cast up hands to the Heavens, and pray without
a word,
As they that have seen God's visage, and the face of the
Father have heard.

They are gone—the lovely, the mighty, the hope of the
ancient Earth:
It shall labour and bear the burden as before that day of
their birth: 330
It shall groan in its blind abiding for the day that Sigurd
hath sped,
And the hour that Brynhild hath hastened, and the dawn
that waketh the dead:
It shall yearn, and be oft-times holpen, and forget their
deeds no more,
Till the new sun beams on Baldur, and the happy sealess
shore.

From The House of the Wolfings

Tidings of the Battle in Mirkwood.

...Then he set down the horn and spake:

'We, the Shieldings, with the Geirings, the Hrossings, and the Wolfings, three hundred warriors and more, were led into the Wood by Thiodolf the War-duke, beside whom went Fox, who had seen the Romans. We were all afoot; 5 for there is no wide way through the Wood, nor would we have it otherwise, lest the foe find the thicket easy. But many of us know the thicket and its ways; so we made not the easy hard. I was near the War-duke, for I know the thicket and am light-foot: I am a bowman. I 10 saw Thiodolf that he was unhelmed and bore no shield, nor had he any coat of fence; nought but a deer-skin frock.... Yet by his side was his mighty sword, and we all knew it for Throng-plough, and were glad of it and of him and the unfenced breast of the dauntless. Six hours 15 we went spreading wide through the thicket, not always seeing one another, but knowing one another to be nigh; those that knew the thicket best led, the others followed on. So we went till it was high noon on the plain and glimmering dusk in the thicket, and we saw nought, save 20 here and there a roe, and here and there a sounder of swine, and coneys where it was opener, and the sun shone and the grass grew for a little space. So came we unto where the thicket ended suddenly, and there was a long glade of the wild-wood, all set about with great oak-trees and grass 25 thereunder, which I knew well; and thereof the tale tells that it was a holy place of the folk who abided in these parts before the Sons of the Goths. Now will I drink.'

So he drank of the horn and said: 'It seemeth that Fox had a deeming of the way the Romans should come; so 30 now we abided in the thicket without that glade and lay

149

quiet and hidden, spreading ourselves as much about that lawn of the oak-trees as we might, the while Fox and three others crept through the wood to espy what might be toward: not long had they been gone ere we heard a war- 35 horn blow, and it was none of our horns: it was a long way off, but we looked to our weapons: for men are eager for the foe and the death that cometh, when they lie hidden in the thicket. A while passed, and again we heard the horn, and it was nigher and had a marvellous voice; then 40 in a while was a little noise of men, not their voices, but footsteps going warily through the brake to the south, and twelve men came slowly and warily into that oak-lawn, and lo, one of them was Fox; but he was clad in the raiment of the dastard of the Goths whom he had slain. I tell you 45 my heart beat, for I saw that the others were Roman men, and one of them seemed to be a man of authority, and he held Fox by the shoulder, and pointed to the thicket where we lay, and something he said to him, as we saw by his gesture and face, but his voice we heard not, for he spake 50 soft.

'Then of those ten men of his he sent back two, and Fox going between them, as though he should be slain if he misled them; and he and the eight abided there wisely and warily, standing silently some six feet from each other, 55 moving scarce at all, but looking like images fashioned of brown copper and iron; holding their casting-spears (which be marvellous heavy weapons) and girt with the sax.

'As they stood there, not out of earshot of a man speaking in his wonted voice, our War-duke made a sign to those 60 about him, and we spread very quietly to the right hand and the left of him once more, and we drew as close as might be to the thicket's edge, and those who had bows the nighest thereto. Thus then we abided a while again; and again came the horn's voice; for belike they had no 65 mind to come their ways covertly because of their pride.

'Soon therewithal comes Fox creeping back to us, and I saw him whisper into the ear of the War-duke, but heard not the word he said. I saw that he had hanging to him two Roman saxes, so I deemed he had slain those two, and so escaped the Romans. Maidens, it were well that ye gave me to drink again, for I am weary and my journey is done.' 70

So again they brought him the horn, and made much of him; and he drank, and then spake on. 75

'Now heard we the horn's voice again quite close, and it was sharp and shrill, and nothing like to the roar of our battle-horns: still was the wood and no wind abroad, not even down the oak-lawn; and we heard now the tramp of many men as they thrashed through the small wood and bracken of the thicket-way; and those eight men and their leader came forward, moving like one, close up to the thicket where I lay, just where the path passed into the thicket beset by the Sons of the Goths: so near they were that I could see the dints upon their armour, and the strands of the wire on their sax-handles. Down then bowed the tall bracken on the further side of the wood-lawn, the thicket crashed before the march of men, and on they strode into the lawn, a goodly band, wary, alert, and silent of cries. ... 80 85 90

'There they stayed awhile, and spread out but a little, as men marching, not as men fighting. A while we let them be; and we saw their captain, no big man, but dight with very fair armour and weapons. ...

'The prey had come into the net, but they had turned their faces toward the mouth of it. 95

'Then turned Thiodolf swiftly to the man behind him who carried the war-horn, and every man handled his weapons: but that man understood, and set the little end

151

to his mouth, and loud roared the horn of the Markmen, 100
and neither friend nor foe misdoubted the tale thereof.
Then leaped every man to his feet, all bow-strings twanged
and the cast-spears flew; no man forbore to shout; each
as he might leapt out of the thicket and fell on with sword
and axe and spear, for it was from the bowmen but one 105
shaft and no more.

'Then might you have seen Thiodolf as he bounded
forward like the wild-cat on the hare, how he had no eyes
for any save the Roman captain. Foemen enough he had
round him after the two first bounds from the thicket; for 110
the Romans were doing their best to spread, that they
might handle those heavy cast-spears, though they might
scarce do it, just come out of the thicket as they were, and
thrust together by that onslaught of the kindreds falling
on from two sides and even somewhat from behind. To 115
right and left flashed Throng-plough, while Thiodolf
himself scarce seemed to guide it: men fell before him at
once...and in a minute of time was he amidst of the throng
and face to face with the gold-dight captain.

'What with the sweep of Throng-plough and the 120
Wolfing onrush, there was space about him for a great
stroke; he gave a side-long stroke to his right and hewed
down a tall Burgundian, and then up sprang the white
blade, but ere its edge fell he turned his wrist, and drove the
point through that Captain's throat just above the ending 125
of his hauberk, so that he fell dead amidst of his folk.

'All the four kindreds were on them now, and amidst
them, and needs must they give way: but stoutly they
fought; for surely no other warriors might have withstood
that onslaught of the Markmen for the twinkling of an eye: 130
but had the Romans had but the space to have spread
themselves out there, so as to handle their shot weapons,
many a woman's son of us had fallen; for no man shielded

himself in his eagerness, but let the swiftness of the onset
of point-and-edge shield him; which, sooth to say, is often 135
a good shield, as here was found.

'So those that were unslain and unhurt fled west along
the glade, but not as dastards, and had not Thiodolf
followed hard in the chase according to his wont, they
might even yet have made a fresh stand and spread from 140
oak-tree to oak-tree across the glade: but as it befell, they
might not get a fair offing so as to disentangle themselves
and array themselves in good order side by side; and
whereas the Markmen were fleet of foot, and in the woods
they knew, there were a many Aliens slain in the chase 145
or taken alive unhurt or little hurt: but the rest fled this
way and that way into the thicket, with whom were some
of the Burgundians; so there they abide now as outcasts
and men unholy, to be slain as wild-beasts one by one as
we meet them.   150

'Such then was the battle in Mirkwood. Give me the
mead-horn that I may drink to the living and the dead,
and the memory of the dead, and the deeds of the living
that are to be.'

So they brought him the horn, and he waved it over his 155
head and drank again. . . .

From The Story of the Glittering Plain
Of the Fight of the Champions

. . .Now when the folk saw him, and how slim and light
and small he looked beside their champion, and they beheld
the Raven painted on his white shield, they hooted and
laughed for scorn of him and his littleness. But he tossed
his sword up lightly and caught it by the hilts as it fell, 5
and drew nigher to the champion of the sea and stood

153

facing him within reach of his sword. Then the chieftain on the high-seat put his two hands to his mouth and roared out: 'Fall on, ye champions, fall on!'

But the folk in the hall were so eager that they stood 10 on the benches and the boards, and craned over each other's shoulders, so that they might lose no whit of the hand-play. Now flashed the blades in the candle-lit hall, and the red-haired champion hove up his sword and smote two great strokes to right and to left; but the alien gave 15 way before him, and the folk cried out at him in scorn and in joy of their champion, who fell to raining down great strokes like the hail amidst the lightning. But so deft was the alien, that he stood amidst it unhurt, and laid many strokes on his foeman, and did all so lightly and 20 easily, that it seemed as if he were dancing rather than fighting; and the folk held their peace and began to doubt if their huge champion would prevail. Now the red-haired fetched a mighty stroke at the alien, who leapt aside lightly and gat his sword in his left hand and dealt a great 25 stroke on the other's head, and the red-haired staggered, for he had over-reached himself; and again the alien smote him a left-handed stroke so that he fell full length on the floor with a mighty clatter, and the sword flew out of his hand: and the folk were dumb-founded.... 30

From News From Nowhere

I

WORKERS

We came just here on a gang of men road-mending, which delayed us a little; but I was not sorry for it; for all I had seen hitherto seemed a mere part of a summer holiday, and I wanted to see how this folk would set to on a piece of real, necessary work. They had been resting, 5 and had only just begun work again as we came up; so that the rattle of the picks was what woke me from my musing. There were about a dozen of them, strong young men, looking much like a boating party at Oxford would have looked in the days I remembered, and not more troubled with their work: their outer raiment lay on the road-side in an orderly pile under the guardianship of a six-year-old boy, who had his arm thrown over the neck of a big mastiff, who was as happily lazy as if the summer day had been made for him alone. As I eyed the pile of clothes, I could see the gleam of gold and silk embroidery on it.... Beside them lay a good big basket that had hints about it of cold pie and wine; a half dozen of young women stood by watching the work or the workers, both of which were worth watching, for the latter smote great strokes and were very deft in their labour, and as handsome clean-built fellows as you might find a dozen of in a summer day. They were laughing and talking merrily with each other and the women, but presently their foreman looked up and saw our way stopped. So he stayed his pick and sang out, 'Spell ho, mates! here are neighbours want to get past.' Whereon the others stopped also, and, drawing around us, helped the old horse by easing our wheels over the half undone road, and then, like men with a pleasant task on hand, hurried back to their work, only stopping to give us a smiling good-day; so that the sound of the picks broke out again before Graylocks had taken to his jog-trot. Dick looked back over his shoulder at them and said:

'They are in luck to-day: it's right down good sport trying how much pick-work one can get into an hour; and I can see those neighbours know their business well. It is not a mere matter of strength getting on quickly with such work, is it, Guest?'

155

'I should think not,' said I, 'but to tell you the truth, 40
I have never tried my hand at it.'

'Really?' said he gravely, 'that seems a pity; it is good
work for hardening the muscles, and I like it; though I
admit it is pleasanter the second week than the first. Not
that I am a good hand at it: the fellows used to chaff me 45
at one job where I was working, I remember, and sing out
to me, "Well rowed, stroke!" "Put your back into it,
bow!"'

'Not much of a joke,' quoth I.

'Well,' said Dick, 'everything seems like a joke when 50
we have a pleasant spell of work on, and good fellows
merry about us; we feel so happy, you know.' Again I
pondered silently.

II

KELMSCOTT

The raised way led us into a little field bounded by a
backwater of the river on one side, on the right hand we 55
could see a cluster of small houses and barns, new and old,
and before us a grey stone barn and a wall partly overgrown
with ivy, over which a few grey gables showed. The
village road ended in the shallow of the aforesaid backwater.
We crossed the road, and again almost without my will 60
my hand raised the latch of a door in the wall, and we
stood presently on a stone path which led up to the old
house to which fate in the shape of Dick had so strangely
brought me in this new world of men. My companion
gave a sigh of pleased surprise and enjoyment; nor did I 65
wonder, for the garden between the wall and the house
was redolent of the June flowers, and the roses were rolling
over one another with that delicious superabundance of
small well-tended gardens which at first sight takes away
all thought from the beholder save that of beauty. The 70

blackbirds were singing their loudest, the doves were cooing on the roof-ridge, the rooks in the high elm-trees beyond were garrulous among the young leaves, and the swifts wheeled whining about the gables. And the house itself was a fit guardian for all the beauty of this heart of 75 summer.

Once again Ellen echoed my thoughts as she said: 'Yes, friend, this is what I came out for to see; this many-gabled old house built by the simple country-folk of the long-past times, regardless of all the turmoil that was going on in 80 cities and courts, is lovely still amidst all the beauty which these latter days have created; and I do not wonder at our friends tending it carefully and making much of it. It seems to me as if it had waited for these happy days, and held in it the gathered crumbs of happiness of the confused 85 and turbulent past.'

She led me up close to the house, and laid her shapely sun-browned hand and arm on the lichened wall as if to embrace it, and cried out, 'O me! O me! How I love the earth, and the seasons, and weather, and all things that deal 90 with it, and all that grows out of it,—as this has done!'

I could not answer her, or say a word. Her exultation and pleasure were so keen and exquisite, and her beauty, so delicate, yet so interfused with energy, expressed it so fully, that any added word would have been commonplace 95 and futile. I dreaded lest the others should come in suddenly and break the spell she had cast about me; but we stood there a while by the corner of the big gable of the house, and no one came. I heard the merry voices some way off presently, and knew that they were going along 100 the river to the great meadow on the other side of the house and garden.

We drew back a little, and looked up at the house: the door and the windows were open to the fragrant sun-cured

air; from the upper window-sills hung festoons of flowers 105
in honour of the festival, as if the others shared in the love
for the old house.

'Come in,' said Ellen. 'I hope nothing will spoil it
inside, but I don't think it will. Come! we must go back
presently to the others. They have gone on to the tents; 110
for surely they must have tents pitched for the haymakers—
the house would not hold a tithe of the folk, I am sure.'

She led me on to the door, murmuring a little above her
breath as she did so, 'The earth, and the growth of it and
the life of it. If I could but say or show how I love it.' 115

We went in, and found no soul in any room as we
wandered from room to room,—from the rose-covered
porch to the strange and quaint garrets amongst the great
timbers of the roof, where of old time the tillers and herds-
men of the manor slept, but which a-nights seemed now, 120
by the small size of the beds, and the litter of useless and
disregarded matters—bunches of dying flowers, feathers of
birds, shells of starling's eggs, caddis worms in mugs, and
the like—seemed to be inhabited for the time by children.

Everywhere there was but little furniture, and that only 125
the most necessary, and of the simplest forms. The
extravagant love of ornament which I had noted in this
people elsewhere seemed here to have given place to the
feeling that the house itself and its associations was the
ornament of the country life amidst which it had been left 130
stranded from old times, and that to re-ornament it would
but take away its use as a piece of natural beauty.

We sat down at last in a room over the wall which
Ellen had caressed, and which was still hung with old
tapestry, originally of no artistic value, but now faded into 135
pleasant grey tones which harmonised thoroughly well
with the quiet of the place, and which would have been
ill supplanted by brighter and more striking decoration.

The Burghers' Battle

Thick rise the spear-shafts o'er the land
That erst the harvest bore;
The sword is heavy in the hand,
And we return no more.

The light wind waves the Ruddy Fox,   5
Our banner of the war,
And ripples in the Running Ox,
And we return no more.

Across our stubble acres now,
The teams go four and four;   10
But out-worn elders guide the plough,
And we return no more.

And now the women heavy-eyed
Turn through the open door
From gazing down the highway wide,   15
Where we return no more.

The shadows of the fruited close
Dapple the feast-hall floor;
There lie our dogs and dream and doze,
And we return no more.   20

Down from the minster tower to-day
Fall the soft chimes of yore
Amidst the chattering jackdaws' play:
And we return no more.

But underneath the streets are still;   25
Noon, and the market's o'er!
Back go the goodwives o'er the hill;
For we return no more.

What merchants to our gates shall come?
What wise man bring us lore? 30
What abbot ride away to Rome,
Now we return no more?

What mayor shall rule the hall we built?
Whose scarlet sweep the floor?
What judge shall doom the robber's guilt, 35
Now we return no more?

New houses in the street shall rise
Where builded we before,
Of other stone wrought otherwise;
For we return no more. 40

And crops shall cover field and hill
Unlike what once they bore,
And all be done without our will,
Now we return no more.

Look up! the arrows streak the sky, 45
The horns of battle roar;
The long spears lower and draw nigh,
And we return no more.

Remember how beside the wain
We spoke the word of war, 50
And sowed this harvest of the plain,
And we return no more.

Lay spears about the Ruddy Fox!
The days of old are o'er;
Heave sword about the Running Ox! 55
For we return no more.

Iceland First Seen

Lo from our loitering ship
a new land at last to be seen;
Toothed rocks down the side of the firth
on the east guard a weary wide lea,
And black slope the hillsides above,   5
striped adown with their desolate green:
And a peak rises up on the west
from the meeting of cloud and of sea,
Foursquare from base unto point
like the building of Gods that have been,   10
The last of that waste of the mountains
all cloud-wreathed and snow-flecked and grey,
And bright with the dawn that began
just now at the ending of day.

Ah! what came we forth for to see   15
that our hearts are so hot with desire?
Is it enough for our rest,
the sight of this desolate strand,
And the mountain-waste voiceless as death
but for winds that may sleep not nor tire?   20
Why do we long to wend forth
through the length and breadth of a land,
Dreadful with grinding of ice,
and record of scarce hidden fire,
But that there 'mid the grey grassy dales   25
sore scarred by the ruining streams
Lives the tale of the Northland of old
and the undying glory of dreams?

O land, as some cave by the sea
where the treasures of old have been laid,   30

The sword it may be of a king
whose name was the turning of fight:
Or the staff of some wise of the world
that many things made and unmade,
Or the ring of a woman, maybe,   35
whose woe is grown wealth and delight.
No wheat and no wine grows above it,
no orchard for blossom and shade;
The few ships that sail by its blackness
but deem it the mouth of a grave;   40
Yet sure when the world shall awaken,
this too shall be mighty to save.

Or rather, O land, if a marvel
it seemeth that ever men sought
Thy wastes for a field and a garden   45
fulfilled of all wonder and doubt,
And feasted amidst of the winter
when the fight of the year had been fought,
Whose plunder all gathered together
was little to babble about;   50
Cry aloud from thy wastes, O thou land,
'Not for this nor for that was I wrought.
Amid waning of realms and their riches
and death of things worshipped and sure,
I abide here the spouse of a God,   55
and I made and I make and I endure.'

O Queen of the grief without knowledge,
of the courage that may not avail,
Of the longing that may not attain,
of the love that shall never forget,   60
More joy than the gladness of laughter
thy voice hath amidst of its wail:

More hope than of pleasure fulfilled
amidst of thy blindness is set ;
More glorious than gaining of all   65
thine unfaltering hand that shall fail :
For what is the mark on thy brow
but the brand that thy Brynhild doth bear ?
Lone once, and loved and undone
by a love that no ages outwear.   70

Ah ! when thy Balder comes back,
and bears from the heart of the Sun
Peace and the healing of pain,
and the wisdom that waiteth no more ;
And the lilies are laid on thy brow   75
'mid the crown of the deeds thou hast done ;
And the roses spring up by thy feet
that the rocks of the wilderness wore :
Ah ! when thy Balder comes back
and we gather the gains he hath won,   80
Shall we not linger a little
to talk of thy sweetness of old,
Yea, turn back awhile to thy travail
whence the Gods stood aloof to behold ?

The Flowering Orchard

SILK EMBROIDERY

Lo silken my garden,
and silken my sky,
And silken my apple-boughs
hanging on high ;
All wrought by the Worm   5
in the peasant carle's cot
On the Mulberry leafage
when summer was hot !

For a Bed

The wind's on the wold
And the night is acold,
And Thames runs chill
'Twixt mead and hill,
But kind and dear   5
Is the old house here,
And my heart is warm
'Midst winter's harm.

Rest then and rest,
And think of the best   10
'Twixt summer and spring
When all birds sing
In the town of the tree,
And ye lie in me
And scarce dare move,   15
Lest earth and its love
Should fade away
Ere the full of the day.

I am old and have seen
Many things that have been;   20
Both grief and peace
And wane and increase.
No tale I tell
Of ill or well,
But this I say,   25
Night treadeth on day,
And for worst and best
Right good is rest.

NOTES

ROSSETTI

THE BLESSED DAMOZEL

Written in early youth and first published in *The Germ*. It was constantly revised, and the alterations shed interesting light on the poet's development. For a summary see *Dante Gabriel Rossetti* by William Sharp, Chapter V.

19. *ten years of years*: to the lover on earth each year seemed as long as many years.

44. *circling charm*: the "gold bar of Heaven," as well as the mystic limit which may not be passed.

63. *Fain*: the 'Pre-Raphaelite' poets consistently used this word in the sense of 'anxious' or 'willing.'

71. *two prayers*: Matthew xviii. 19: "If two of you shall agree on earth as touching anything that they shall ask, it shall be done for them."

76. *deep wells of light*: this, like the "white raiment" in l. 74, and the lamps, the mystic tree and the Dove in later stanzas, is an echo of *Revelations*.

90. *Saith His name audibly*: possibly *Sanctus Spiritus* is suggested, which 'imitates' the sound of rustling wings.

126. *citherns and citoles*: both (from Lat. *cithara*) were obsolete instruments like the modern zither. The citole belongs more accurately to the Dantesque period to which the poem would seem to apply than the cithern, which was popular during the 16th and 17th centuries.

THE STAFF AND SCRIP

54. *grame*: sorrow, ill-hap.

70. *scrip*: a pilgrim's small bag or wallet.

76. *wrought*: embroidered.

77. *one white lily*: the Queen's name was Blanche-lys.

156 to the end. The Queen has died, and here the poet is addressing the shade of the Knight in Heaven, where he appears (as in mediaeval legend) in armour. The Queen is now his— "God pays the wage he owed"—and there is no deduction from the reward, no 'tithe' kept back. So is the pilgrim repaid for keeping his oath on earth.

THE PORTRAIT

This is another of the early poems, and is not 'autobiographical.' Benson sees in it traces of Tennyson, and adds: "If I had to select one poem of Rossetti's to illustrate the early simple manner at its very best, I should certainly choose *The Portrait*. It is worth noting that the third stanza was chosen by Buchanan as an example of Rossetti's 'slovenly writing.'"

26. *And your own footsteps meeting you.* Rossetti painted a picture, "How they met themselves," embodying this same idea. It is the old German legend of the "Döppelgänger."

SISTER HELEN

Rossetti himself called this "the pitch of brutal bogyism." The magic element in it is a world-wide legend, that if you wished to destroy your enemy you made a waxen image of him, recited over it certain spells, and placed it before the fire. As the image melted, so your enemy, wherever he might be, would sicken, and finally, with the complete collapse of the image, die.

Rossetti thought the poem "a not unfair exercise" for the reader's comprehension, but wrote the earlier stanzas to help the less ingenious. The difficulties tend to disappear as one reads it more often, but it may be as well to know beforehand that Sister Helen (whom we may presume to be a wealthy orphan, since she lives in a castle and has no knight to avenge her) has been betrayed by Keith of Ewern, whose relatives ride to her castle to plead for his life.

141. *a ring and a broken coin*: referring to the custom of breaking a coin on parting, each half to be kept (as also the ring) as a pledge, and to be returned in times of danger or anxiety.

169–197. Between these stanzas later editions of the poem contained six more, in which Sir Keith's bride also appears at the castle to plead for him. See Sharp, *ut supra*.

179. *Fire shall forgive*: i.e. the only forgiveness he can expect from me is that which I shall receive from the fires of Hell.

235. *A soul that's lost*: her own soul is damned for her witchcraft.

THE STREAM'S SECRET

"'The stream is at once the lover's sphinx-like confidant and also a symbol of the progress of love. It will not tell him when, or whether, love's hour shall come to him again, as in imagination he figures it coming. Love stands at the well-head, and sends the enigmatic message down-stream; and 'love's hour' is further imagined as watching its own shadow nearing it upon a dial. Only the hour of parting is certain. But shall there ever be a meeting first? The whispering answer of the water is doubtful." (Oliver Elton.)

BALLAD OF DEAD LADIES

From the French of Villon (15th century). Swinburne, in translating Villon's Ballads, deliberately omitted this one, saying that no man could improve on this version.

1. "'Way,' in which one might actually chance to meet her; the unmistakably poetic effect of the couplet in English being dependent on the definiteness of that single word (though actually lighted on in the search after a difficult double rhyme) for which everyone else would have written, like Villon himself, a more general one, just equivalent to place or region." (Walter Pater.) The original is:

> *Dictes-moy où, n'en quel pays*
> *Est Flora, la belle Romaine.*

2. *Flora*: a Roman courtesan.

3. *Hipparchia*: wife of the cynic philosopher Crates, who embraced the life of abstinence out of love for her husband. Villon has 'Archipiada.'

Thaïs. See Dryden's *Alexander's Feast*.

9. *Héloïse and Abélard* (the usual spelling). Famous mediaeval lovers. Abélard was a popular 'schoolman' and teacher of the 12th century. Héloïse bore him a son and, although after their marriage he forced her to become a nun, she loved him until her death.

12. *dule and teen*: grief and suffering.

14. *Buridan*: a 14th-century French philosopher. There is much doubt as to the Queen's identity. The story ran that she lured young students to her palace and afterwards, in order that

they might not be seen to leave her presence, had them tied in a sack and thrown into the Seine from her windows.

17. *Blanche* : may be any of three or four famous and beautiful Blanches, Queens of mediaeval France.

19. *Bertha Broadfoot*: mother of Charlemagne, called, because of a club-foot, Berthe au Grand-Pied.

Beatrice : Dante's mistress.

Alice : perhaps Alix de Champagne (died 1216), wife of Louis le Jeune of France.

20. *Ermengarde*: Queen of Provence in the 9th century. Villon has 'Harembourges,' more accurately 'the lady of Maine,' since she was daughter of a Count of Maine in the 12th century.

MY FATHER'S CLOSE

The exactness with which Rossetti has 'caught' the original may be gathered from the first stanza in French :

> Au jardin de mon père,
> (*Vole, mon cœur, vole !*)
> Il y a un pommier doux,
> Tout doux.

THE WOODSPURGE

In the moment of agony the poet finds himself gazing intently at a patch of about ten little weeds. The detail impresses itself on his mind and stands out, as inconsequential details often do in moments of high tension, with a sort of hysterical insistence. Literature holds many parallel examples ; perhaps the most entertaining is that of the soldier in *Ravenshoe*, waiting for the order to charge, who can think only of a grease-stain on a comrade's uniform in front of him, and is obsessed with its resemblance to the map of Sweden.

The woodspurge is one of a family of spurges that has greenish-yellow flowers. It is called 'unsavourie' in Gerard's *Herbal* (1597), a book with which Rossetti was familiar from childhood. It is possible (if a little unkind) to believe that it was there, and not in a moment of agony, that Rossetti discovered that "the woodspurge has a cup of three."

THE WHITE SHIP

Note, in this ballad, how the style is not consistently simple ; it sometimes becomes more characteristic of Rossetti than of the "butcher of Rouen."

168

14. *Clerkly Harry* : Henry I was called Beauclerc.

226. *daïs* : a monosyllable here, as always with Swinburne and Morris.

234. *rede* : as meaning ' narrative this is rare, if correct. The usual meaning is 'counsel,' as in Ethelred the Unready, *i.e.* the redeless.

SOOTHSAY

This contains a statement of Rossetti's faith, or rather his creed. Like many of these non-lyrical lyrics, it needs to be read slowly and carefully.

10–14. *the dust*, etc. Compare Hamlet's speech at the grave-side ; or, finer still, John Donne's *Sermons* : "as soon the dust of a wretch whom thou wouldest not, as of a Prince thou couldest not look upon, shall trouble thine eyes if the wind blow it thither."

THE CLOUD CONFINES

Another expression of faith—or lack of faith. Among the fragments collected by Rossetti's brother for inclusion in the Collected Works are two lines with a similar thought :

> Would God I knew there were a God to thank
> When thanks arise in me !

19. *Whether they two were we* : another echo of the Döppelgänger legend, as in *The Portrait*, and " How They Met Themselves."

HAND AND SOUL

Chiaro dell' Erma, having painted beautiful pictures that were popular, and religious pictures that were not, watches from his window a fight between rival factions, during which the frescoes which he had painted in the church porch are ruined by blood-stains. He is in despair, believing that Fame and Faith have both failed him. His soul appears to him in a vision and inspires him to paint her, and the work fills discerning men to this day with awe and fear.

The moral—the necessity for sincerity—appears again with qualifications in another story (unfinished) by the poet, called *The St Agnes of Intercession* : " It has seemed to me that all work, to be truly worthy, should be wrought out of the age itself, as well as out of the soul of its producer...."

Hand and Soul first appeared in *The Germ* and was included, with many alterations, in the Collected Works.

WILLIAM MORRIS

FRANK'S SEALED LETTER

One of Morris's few and unsuccessful attempts to write a story of his own times. The opening paragraph, given here, offers an excellent defence of his own early indecision.

A GOOD KNIGHT IN PRISON

36. *castellan* : Governor of the castle.

40–45. This is Morris, rather than Sir Guy, who speaks.

91. *Mahound* : a corruption of Mahommed.

104. *la perrière* : an instrument for slinging great stones.

THE GILLIFLOWER OF GOLD

1. *gilliflower* : the pink, or clove-pink.

30. *tabard* : a short cloak, open at the sides.

THE EVE OF CRECY

4. *The refrain.* It is not fanciful here to catch the note of Chaucer and the early French romances—"*si douce est la marguerite.*"

14. *arrière-ban* : the order of a French king summoning his vassals to war.

15. *basnet* : a kind of helmet.

34. *this battle* : the young French knight is quite confident of victory on the morrow and hopes to catch the King's eye.

46. *banneret* : originally a knight who brought his own troops under his own banner ; but later, as here, the title was reserved for those who performed valiant deeds in the King's presence.

THE JUDGMENT OF GOD

The title was the old name for trial by single combat.

14. *that wrong*: Son Roger—and perhaps his father—had cut down a woman from the stake where she was to be burnt (ll. 66 etc.) and killed her enemy, cutting off his hands and bearing his severed head on his spear-point (ll. 20–23). This treatment was reserved for commoners, and hence Roger admits "that wrong."

29. *White linen*: to signify that his cause was pure.

THE HAYSTACK IN THE FLOODS

52. *the Châtelet*: there was an ancient fortress of that name in Paris which was pulled down in 1802.

153. *fitte*: ironic. The fytte was the stanza or division of mediaeval romances.

THE LIFE AND DEATH OF JASON

1. *the Minyae*: the Argonauts, so named from Minyas, king of the country whence they came.

27. *The wise king's bird*: the dove, given to the Argonauts by Phineus, King of Salmydessa, whom they had delivered from the torments of the Harpies. If the dove successfully passed through the Symplegades, the Argo would be able to pass through after her.

The Song from Book IV was sung by the nymph to Hylas.

THE EARTHLY PARADISE

PRELUDE

25. *the Ivory Gate*: the gate of dreams unfulfilled. The Gate of Horn admitted those dreams that were to come true.

ATALANTA'S RACE

Atalanta was the daughter of Iasus and Clymene, according to one version; Apollodorus, from whom Morris took his account, makes King Schoenus her father. She was so fleet of foot, and so anxious to remain a virgin, that she made her suitors run

races with her. If they were beaten—as they always were—
they were executed on the spot. Milanion (Hippomenes, in
the other story) having watched one suitor fail, determines to
win her. He departs thoughtfully, 'trains' strictly for the race
and also consults a Goddess, who gives him the three golden
apples which are to prove too much for Atalanta's feminine
heart. Though she loses the race she is happy in her lover.

THE MAN BORN TO BE KING

The legend, from the *Gesta Romanorum*, is of a king who
learns from a prophet that a man, not his own son, shall one
day succeed to his throne. He takes no heed of the prophecy
until, some years later, he outstrips his fellows in the chase and
seeks shelter in a woodman's hut. That night a son is born to
the woodman's wife. The King fears that this is the boy who
is to oust him (possibly by murdering him) and he lays all sorts
of plans to kidnap and destroy him. All his plots fail, and when,
after an adventurous life, the boy eventually marries the King's
daughter—his only child—he sees that it is useless to struggle
against Fate, and is reconciled.

In this extract the boy is on his way to the castle where the
Princess dwells. He bears a letter from the King to the keeper
of the castle with instructions to murder the lad. But he falls
asleep under a tree, where he is discovered by the Princess and
her friend. They steal his letter and substitute for it one which
says that the bearer is the bridegroom whom the King has
chosen for his daughter. The two are married and her father,
coming to visit the castle, is amazed at the effect of his letter.

The present extract is an example of how Morris tides over
what might well have been a dull passage in the story.

L'ENVOI

6. *I love thee*: J. W. Mackail, in his *Life of William Morris*,
describes the author's sadness at having finished *The Earthly
Paradise*.

46. *Geoffrey Chaucer*: *The Earthly Paradise* is written almost
entirely in metres which were favourites of Chaucer.

81. *The House of Fame*: the title of an allegory by Chaucer.

* Poems or passages marked with an asterisk are not printed complete.

39. *midward*: prime; lit., the middle-time.

62. *Signy*: the daughter of Volsung. Siggeir, King of the Goths, had come to ask her in marriage, and she had accepted, knowing that it was the will of the Fates, although she hated him.

130. Siggeir proceeds to beg to be allowed to feel the sword in his hands, but not for a moment will Sigmund relinquish it.

136. *Gripir*: the owner of a famous breed of horses.

139. *Regin*: Sigurd's tutor, an old Merlin-like magician.

209. *the Wrath*: Sigurd's sword.

218. *Fafnir's bane*: *i.e.*, the sword with which he slew Fafnir, the dragon guarding the hoard of gold.

230. *tiles of Odin*: war-shields, Odin being God of War.

305. *bale*: a pile of wood for burning, a pyre.

334. *Balder*: the Scandinavian God of Light, son of Odin and Freya. He was killed by Loki (see Matthew Arnold: *Balder Dead*) with a sprig of mistletoe, this being the only thing omitted by Freya when she bound all things by an oath never to harm Balder. His death was the beginning of the overthrow of the Gods in the period called Ragnarök, the Twilight of the Gods.

When Balder returns with the other sons of Odin he will institute a new and righteous dynasty of Gods.

THE HOUSE OF THE WOLFINGS

1. *Geirings*, etc.: Gothic tribes.

21. *sounder*: herd.

45. *dastard*: craven, or traitor.

58. *sax*: a short dagger or knife.

100. *Markmen*: dwellers in the Mark or march—a border province, probably of the Roman empire.

112. *cast-spears*: presumably small spears for throwing.

123. *Burgundians*: fighting as Roman troops.

THE GLITTERING PLAIN

This was the first book to be printed at the Kelmscott Press.

5. *hilts*: the use of the word in the plural is archaic.

NEWS FROM NOWHERE

Morris's 'Utopia' was a kind of answer to a book published a little earlier in America called *Looking Backward* by one Bellamy. This book, which had had a great vogue, had painted an age of perfected civilisation. *News from Nowhere* is aggressively pastoral.

3. *a summer holiday* : it has been reasonably objected (by Alfred Noyes) that Morris "did subconsciously abolish the seasons from his new Arcadia."

9. *like* : one of Morris's little grammatical uncertainties. Compare *The Judgment of God*, l. 38.

FOR A BED

From the Catalogue of the Fourth Exhibition of the Arts and Crafts Society. Composed for an embroidered hanging around the top of a canopied four-poster bed. The bed was his own—a piece of 17th-century carved oak—and the verses were designed and worked by the poet's daughter, Miss May Morris.

For EU product safety concerns, contact us at Calle de José Abascal, 56–1°,
28003 Madrid, Spain or eugpsr@cambridge.org.

www.ingramcontent.com/pod-product-compliance
Ingram Content Group UK Ltd.
Pitfield, Milton Keynes, MK11 3LW, UK
UKHW040615240426
470322UK00010B/141